Money and Liberty

S. Herbert Frankel

Money and Liberty

S. Herbert Frankel

American Enterprise Institute for Public Policy Research
Washington, D.C.

S. Herbert Frankel was professor of economics and chairman of the Department of Economics and Economic History at the University of the Witwatersrand from 1931 to 1946; professor of the economics of underdeveloped countries at Oxford University from 1946 to 1971; and visiting professor of economics at the University of Virginia in 1967 and from 1969 to 1974. Since 1971 he has been professor emeritus at Oxford University.

Library of Congress Cataloging in Publication Data

Frankel, Sally Herbert, 1903–
   Money and liberty.

   (AEI studies ; 293)
   1. Money. I. Title. II. Series: American Enterprise Institute for Public Policy Research. AEI studies ; 293.
HG221.F836   332.4   80–21118
ISBN 0-8447-3398-9

AEI Studies 293

Printed in the United States of America

To the memory of my colleague
G. Warren Nutter

Contents

Preface

This study deals with the predicament in which the free world finds itself as a result of the moral and political threat to the money economy today. It is a sequel to my book *Two Philosophies of Money*, to which I refer when it is relevant. Whereas the earlier work dealt largely with conceptual issues, in the present study I examine monetary experience, in historical perspective and in relation to the political and moral problems of our time.

I wish to express my indebtedness to the Earhart Foundation for supporting my research in the United States. For valuable encouragement I wish to thank John H. Moore, William Fellner, Gottfried Haberler, and Richard A. Ware.

S. HERBERT FRANKEL
Nuffield College
Oxford
March 1980

1
Trust

In the free world of far-flung commerce and finance the money economy is taken for granted. Why then should anyone be concerned about its future? Have not governments in most countries established machinery to control, regulate, guide, and improve its working? Is not this intricate machinery both a necessary and a sufficient means of protection against monetary excesses? Or should the encroachment of government in monetary affairs in this century be treated with suspicion? Is it a sign of corruption in the body politic or only in the money economy?

These are not idle questions. Indeed, there had even been misgivings three hundred years ago, at the very birth of the public finance and credit system on which modern states were built. There were fears that the new monetary system harbored the seeds of corruption and decay. Were these fears misplaced? Is corruption of the money economy, after all, unavoidable? And in what does that corruption consist? What is responsible for it, and how can it be dealt with?

For the last fifty years there has been very little discussion of such questions. That was far from being the case in the seventeenth and eighteenth centuries. Then there was fierce political debate about them. Why then do we so frequently ignore them now? Have such questions become irrelevant? Or have policy makers merely set their sights on other targets?

I submit that whatever the cause of the neglect of these issues, the terms in which they were earlier debated are significant at this time of world monetary turmoil when the very survival of a free monetary order is threatened.

Money and Civic Life

What do I mean by a free monetary order? I would answer, briefly, that it is one subject to the rule of law and custom and free from arbitrary manipulation by government or political pressure groups. A money economy based on such a monetary order is one of the most subtle forms of civil association and individual freedom. It is a reflection of a way of civic life (some implications of which are examined in my recent book *Two Philosophies of Money: The Conflict of Trust and Authority*[1]).

A money economy is no exception to the fact that all political, economic, or social associations carry with them not only advantages but also burdens, not only rights but also duties. At various stages of their history, different societies have been unready, unable, or unwilling to assume all the burdens or obligations a money economy involves. Societies that once shouldered them are no longer willing to do so, or have been forced to abandon them.

Monetary Systems

It is not by accident that in the fifth century B.C. Piraeus, the port city of Athens, had become the great storehouse of Greece, playing in the Mediterranean world the leading role later played in the "world economy" by London and New York. This was due largely to the scrupulous respect given to private property and monetary discipline. In the case of the Athenians it is worth noting that throughout their long history they never changed the legal title or weight of their money.

Free world money economies have throughout history been the exception rather than the rule. They have been vulnerable to the winds of political change: to the rise and fall of empires. At all times they have been surrounded by much larger, economically underdeveloped, and politically backward regions, which remained outside the orbit of monetary relations or only lightly touched by them.

It is possible that the primitive monetary systems of such regions, based on many different commodities or on precious metals, played a more significant historical role than is usually supposed. Paul Einzig wrote:

> Another instance in which primitive money is believed to have played a historical part is that of Sparta. Beyond doubt,

[1] S. Herbert Frankel, *Two Philosophies of Money: The Conflict of Trust and Authority* (New York: St. Martin's Press, 1978).

the choice of iron bars as currency made for isolationism not only commercially but also politically, and this again may possibly have been to some degree at any rate responsible for the Peloponnesian wars which led eventually to the decline of both opponents and of Ancient Greece as a whole. It provided an opportunity for the temporary rise of Macedonia and for the more lasting rise of Rome. Possibly if Sparta had possessed ordinary coined currency, like Athens and the rest of Greece, she might have developed also in other respects on lines similar to those of Athens, and there might have been no irreconcilable contrast between the Spartan and Athenian mentality, a contrast which accounted partly for the hatred with which the Peloponnesian wars were fought to the bitter end.

Einzig continues with a striking example of the way in which primitive money was related to the decline of Rome:

It provided one of the main causes of the westward surge of the pastoral races which eventually led to the overthrow of the Roman Empire . . . the cause of this westward surge was the lack of adequate grazing land. . . . What is not realized by historians is that the main cause of the inadequacy of the grazing lands during that period in the Asiatic steppes was the extensive use of livestock as a currency by the pastoral peoples.

Any object or material which fulfills the purpose of currency is accumulated. . . . Livestock is apt to be kept in far larger numbers than is necessary for its economic nonmonetary use. The result is that, owing to the monetary use of livestock, grazing land and water supplies are apt to be exhausted much sooner than they would be otherwise. There was undoubtedly method in the apparently senseless sadistic madness of the Mongolian invaders who systematically exterminated the populations of conquered countries in order to turn agricultural land into pasture. This might not have been considered necessary had it not been for the excessive size of livestock kept for monetary requirements.[2]

Ronald J. McKennon estimates that today, in some 150 trading countries:

only about 15 or 20 currencies are used by merchants and manufacturers. These are the convertible currencies of the

---

[2] Paul Einzig, *Primitive Money in Its Ethnological, Historical and Economic Aspects*, 2d ed. (Oxford: Pergamon Press, 1966), pp. 496–97.

major nonsocialist industrial countries of Western Europe, North America, and Japan. Because most countries in the world have inconvertible currencies that are not usable internationally, their foreign trade depends heavily on using convertible currencies provided by others. Among less developed economies, these 15 or 20 convertible currencies from industrial countries are used directly for invoicing and as a means of payment. Among the socialist economies of Eastern Europe and Asia, these same few currencies serve as a numeraire to establish relative commodity values and so function as units of account.[3]

Monetary Roles

It has always been difficult to persuade people that a trustworthy, disciplined monetary system is indispensable for the free unfolding of the extended division of labor on which the growth of world economies depends. It has also been difficult to persuade them that free economic endeavor can be fostered only when there is sufficient security to sustain it. It requires an efficiently administered legal system and a generally accepted moral code to assure that individuals will be able to conduct their activities in an atmosphere of mutual trust.

Since ancient times the expansion and intensity of economic activity have varied in proportion to the extent to which these conditions have been fulfilled. Yet resistance to the full acceptance of this fact continues, not only because of the age-old suspicion of money, particularly of a free monetary exchange economy, but also because of the difficulty of grasping that the growth of social customs and the institutions that guarantee them is a lengthy process of trial and error and that economic progress does not proceed in a straight line.

This view is found in the literature of the latter part of the nineteenth century. It culminated in the theories of the "takeoff" after World War II and is closely related to current conceptions of the role of money. The emphasis, however, has changed. It is now fashionable to assert that, instead of a large injection of capital, all that is needed to ensure rapid economic development is an injection of money. The power of money as an independent entity is considered as limitless as the conflicting demands for its use.

All such theories can be traced to attempts to discover in eco-

---

[3] Ronald J. McKennon, book review in *Journal of Economic Literature*, vol. 16 (December 1978), p. 1470.

nomic history a principle labeled "development." These attempts overlook the causes of the decline of the world economies of antiquity. They also ignore the fact that the highly developed network of commerce and finance in the Middle Ages was undermined by the rise of the national territorial state.

The monetary predicament in which the countries of the free world find themselves is a manifestation of a similar process. One nation-state after another is endeavoring to increase its technical control of the monetary system in the belief that it must be tailored to serve particular goals. This view confuses two modes of conduct, according to Michael Oakeshott, which must not be confused: "that of living together and that of acting together. There is a clear-cut distinction between 'civility,' the political order under law, and an enterprise association, the administered implementation of a predetermined purpose."[4] It also marks the difference between monetary policy in peace and in war. In the conduct of war there is one clear goal—winning it. All other alternative goals of action must be subordinated to the overriding purpose.

It is often far from easy to discern the fundamental changes taking place in a money economy, which are insidious and often long drawn out. The symbols under which men and women develop and operate their social institutions all too frequently cease to reflect reality. Like national flags they come to represent the glories of the past rather than the circumstances of the present.

Symbolism of Money

Money is one such symbol. It is a symbol of trust, and trust is intuitive. Moreover, it is a symbol of action, not of passivity. When we trust someone, we go beyond the mere assessment of probabilities or enumeration of facts. Trust enters when more exact knowledge is not available.

This is illustrated by a story told of the South African diamond magnate Barney Barnato. When he was asked for a loan by a small businessman who had once been in his employ, Barnato gave him the loan, which was repaid on the due date. Two years later Barnato was asked to renew the loan and agreed to do so. It was again repaid on the due date. After another two years had passed, Barnato was again asked to renew the loan. He refused, and the would-be borrower was greatly put out. "Why refuse me?" he expostulated.

---

[4] Michael Oakeshott, *On Human Conduct* (Oxford: Clarendon Press, 1975).

"Have I not repaid you twice on the due date?" "Yes," replied Barnato, "that's the point—I was twice disappointed."

What the story illustrates is that trust can ultimately be verified only by actions or descriptions of alleged actions. That is the social significance of trust, which has been defined as assured reliance on some person or thing; as confident dependence on the character, ability, strength, or truth of someone or something.

Trust in a person is based on the belief that the person will honor an obligation and keep a promise under all circumstances over which he or she has control. It is trust in this sense that binds all contractual relationships. Whether unforeseen circumstances are likely to arise that could prevent the fulfillment of promises or obligations through no fault of the parties concerned is a question not of trust but of probability. That is the essential difference between a debt and an investment. The former involves a promise, the latter only the expectation of a return.

Trust or mistrust rests on our idea of the nature or character of a person or body of persons or of a social institution, such as the government. Trust is like love. To attempt to obtain it by bribery or purchase is to debase, indeed to destroy it. When we trust someone, we assume that person will not be false to that trust. That assumption is based on our assessment of the kind of person he or she appears to be or is supposed to be or the customary role that person fulfills.

In a letter dated November 1, 1787, Thomas Jefferson wrote to W. Smith that "a lively sense of filial duty is more effectually impressed on the mind of a son or daughter by reading *King Lear*, than by all the dry volumes of ethics and divinity that ever were written."[5] Immanuel Kant noted that general precepts learned from priests or philosophers are never so efficacious as an example of virtue or holiness because we cannot do without intuitions to verify our concepts. Examples of such concepts are often taken from history or literature and open up a different field of imagination and experience than do pure concepts of the understanding.

The social order and mores that trust in money has reflected in the past have been affected by the rise and fall of nations and empires and world economies, by political changes and social upheavals. That is why the issues raised in the introduction to this essay transcend mere monetary techniques. For money symbolizes the very matrix of society—the trust or mistrust by which the personal and

---

[5] Quoted by Hannah Arendt, "Trust and Politics," in Peter Laslett and W. G. Runciman, eds., *Philosophy, Politics and Society*, 3d series (Oxford: Basil Blackwell, 1969), p. 120.

political interrelations of its members stand or fall. Once trust in money has been lost through whatever circumstances, the freedom of the men and women in society will be correspondingly diminished or ultimately destroyed.

Twentieth-Century Experience

It has usually been assumed that the very existence of money presupposes a freely functioning economy, but the experience of the twentieth century shows otherwise. What diverted attention from the real implications of that experience was a preoccupation with the analysis of statistical aggregates, a consequence of the striking progress made in the exact sciences, particularly the physical sciences, through invention and technology.

This preoccupation led to a subtle but pervasive change in the way social and economic questions and monetary thought and policy came to be examined. Highly sophisticated models were developed to portray and analyze the working of the money economy, and eventually they were used to regulate it in pursuit of national and social objectives. It is not difficult to view the whole apparatus of modern monetary management as mirroring the scientific and technical vision of our age.

In consequence, issues that cannot be readily expressed in abstract models of monetary behavior are overlooked or ignored. To do so, however, is to misconceive the significance both of the historical development of money and of the logic of its institutional role.

Abstraction

One of the most serious of these misconceptions arose from the abstract characteristics that money unavoidably possesses. Abstraction is the Achilles' heel of advanced monetary systems. It causes money to be regarded as exercising powers of its own—powers that individuals possessing it can allegedly wield irrespective of political, social, and economic circumstances. But actually money has no such independent powers: it merely reflects cost and value relationships in the present and expectations concerning them in the future. Governments and individuals are always tempted to resist reality by overlooking or ignoring the inescapable fact that money in itself is nothing, that to be of value it must be translated into specific ends and into concrete objects or services.

Money thus portrays the character of society, the nature of its

7

social and economic relations, which are always based on trust. The more intricate and complex those relations are, the greater must be the trust on which they rest; the further they are extended over time and space, the further also must trust extend. That is why in an expanding world economy the importance of money as an international standard of value must also expand. Similarly, a reliable standard in which long-term debts can be expressed is indispensable for the growth of capital. We cannot, however, seek in money the power to deliver what is beyond its province.

The rise and fall of currencies that in their times played a world-encompassing role were not merely the result of economic circumstances or of political fortune but were also greatly influenced by the way in which the functions of money were conceived. It should occasion no surprise that, wherever trust in money is regarded as of no consequence, law and custom do little to ensure trust in it at home or to extend that trust abroad.

Keynes and Monetary Policy

It is difficult for anyone who did not witness, as I did, the monetary events immediately after World War I to appreciate the great change since then in our beliefs and practices concerning the functions of money. Perhaps only Keynes had a presentiment of the fateful implications of that change. He sensed that a new monetary world was in the making. It might be more accurate to say that he saw that the old world was dying and took it upon himself to be the midwife of the new.

In *A Tract on Monetary Reform*,[6] which he completed in 1923, Keynes presented an unsurpassed analysis of the blow delivered by postwar inflation to the monetary stability that had prevailed in Europe for most of the nineteenth century.

The disintegration of the European currencies made so great an impact on Keynes and his contemporaries that it colored his outlook throughout his career. Keynes was convinced that the prime objective of monetary policy should be to prevent a recurrence of the monetary instability that Europe was then experiencing. The raging inflation of the period had produced vast social and economic changes because, he believed, "Money is only important for what it will procure."[7]

---

[6] John Maynard Keynes, *A Tract on Monetary Reform* (London: Macmillan, 1923).

[7] Ibid., p. 1.

According to Keynes, a change in the monetary unit that affected all operations and transactions uniformly would have no consequences. When the value of money changes, however, it does not change equally for all purposes or for the different classes and groups in society. In particular it penalizes the accumulation of capital and its long-term investment, on which the living standards of a growing world population so greatly depend. By its unique effects, inflation

> transfers wealth from one to another, bestows affluence here and embarrassment there and redistributes Fortune's favours so as to frustrate design and disappoint expectations.
>
> The fluctuations in the value of money since 1914 have been on a scale so great as to constitute, with all that they involve, one of the most significant events in the economic history of the modern world. The fluctuation of the standard, whether gold, silver, or paper, has not only been of unprecedented violence, but has been visited on a society of which the economic organisation is more dependent than that of any earlier epoch on the assumption that the standard of value would be moderately stable.[8]

Keynes exposed the deep psychological tensions and hatreds that the depreciation of money brings about. If it proves a gain to the businessman, it also occasions opprobrium. To the consumer, the businessman's exceptional profits appear the cause rather than the consequence of the rise in prices. That is by no means all, for the confidence of the businessman in his role and status is undermined.

> Amidst the rapid fluctuations of his fortunes he himself loses his conservative instincts, begins to think more of large gains of the moment than of the lesser, but permanent, profits of normal business. The welfare of his enterprise in the relatively distant future weighs less with him than before. . . . In his heart he loses his former self-confidence in his relation to society.[9]

But the violent disturbance of the standard of value has the same psychological effects on society itself by obscuring its real situation. For a time one class can benefit surreptitiously at the expense of another. Without knowing it a country can spend in current consumption those savings that it thinks it is investing for the future. The distinction between capital and income is blurred, and in consequence a depreciating currency enables a community to live, unawares, on its

---

[8] Ibid., p. 2.
[9] Ibid., pp. 24–25.

capital. This is precisely our experience today, sixty years after the events to which Keynes was referring.

How has it come about that we are witnessing the ravages of great monetary instability in spite of the establishment of domestic and international machinery for monetary regulation on an unprecedented scale? Much of the regulation was advocated by Keynes himself to prevent a recurrence of Europe's traumatic currency experiences in the 1920s and 1930s. One of Keynes's main conclusions in the *Tract on Monetary Reform* was that these matters could no longer be left unregulated, but that they should and could be made subject to deliberate decision. He wrote:

> We can no longer afford to leave it in the category of which the distinguishing characteristics are possessed in different degrees by the weather, the birth-rate, and the Constitution,—matters which are settled by natural causes, or are the resultant of the separate action of many individuals acting independently, or require a Revolution to change them.[10]

If there were to be controllers, however, who would they be? How would they control the economic weather? Who would control them?

Times have changed. The groups and classes Keynes thought were losers have often become gainers, whether by accident or by social design. But one obstinate fact remains: The uncertainties and fears from which it was hoped we would be freed by a new monetary dispensation are still with us. Indeed the vast malinvestment and waste of resources due to inflationary expedients have continued at a pace far greater than even the most pessimistic thought possible in the first quarter of this century.

It is worth reflecting on the actual extent of the monetary instability by which Keynes was so appalled when, in the same tract, he looked back on the golden age of the nineteenth century:

> During the Napoleonic Wars and the period immediately succeeding them the extreme fluctuation of English prices within a single year was 22 per cent; and the highest price level reached during the first quarter of the nineteenth century, which we used to reckon the most disturbed period of our currency history, was less than double the lowest and with an interval of thirteen years. Compare with this the extraordinary movements of the past nine years.[11]

---

[10] Ibid., p. 40.
[11] Ibid., p. 2.

What were these extraordinary movements? On the average the wholesale price index for the ten years from 1913 to 1923, which included four years of war, rose less than 9 percent per annum. What appalled Keynes seems to have been a rate of inflation to which many countries would now wish they could return. But the scale and degree of our inflationary experience are perhaps not what most distinguish our present monetary concerns from those we have been considering.

At the time Keynes wrote his earlier books, belief in the basic principles of a money economy was widely accepted. In the free market economy, freedom of individual choice and action could be taken for granted. Only ten years later, Keynes could not unequivocally subscribe to that belief; today such a belief cannot be postulated at all. Apparently Keynes did not fully comprehend, even in his later writings, the forces that were undermining the free monetary order or the extent of the attack on individual freedom that they entailed, although in 1937 he became greatly concerned about inflationary effects of the policies being advocated in his name by some of his followers.[12]

---

[12] Gottfried Haberler, *The State of the World Economy and the International Monetary System*, American Enterprise Institute Reprint, no. 92 (Washington, D.C., 1979).

2
Mistrust

Coinage

As far as is known, coinage did not exist before the middle of the seventh century B.C. The question arises why it did not evolve earlier, since the sophisticated trading empires of the Assyrians, Babylonians, Phoenicians, and others had already functioned for centuries. It is a question that has considerable relevance to current monetary issues because it involves the evolution of monetary trust.

The myth has persisted that the long delay must have occurred because the idea of stamping gold and silver pieces with some emblem or effigy, to save time and inconvenience in weighing them and testing their fineness, had to await chance invention by some ruler or merchant of genius. There is little warrant for believing that myth. Our modern ideas of the value of time should not be transposed into descriptions of antiquity. Time did not then have the same importance in the conduct of trade.

One need only consider practices in relatively backward economic regions even now to realize this. The protracted bargaining between buyers and sellers often resembles a public spectacle in which the spectators as well as the parties directly concerned take part. I remember a zealous colonial government department in East Africa that wanted to "protect" peasants in the marketing of their hides and skins. It was hoped to obtain "fairer" prices for them than, it was alleged, were paid by local traders. The government set up special marketing depots at road junctions. The hides and skins were to be graded there, weighed in the presence of inspectors, valued by marketing "experts," and paid for in cash. What could have seemed fairer to any objective mind? Alas, minds work subjectively. It is sad to relate that the number of people availing themselves of these new facilities was minimal. When I asked the peasants why, one of them summed it all up: "It is not enjoyable," he said. "When we come to sell, we like to drink coffee, hear news, listen to dancing records on the gramophone, and laugh with the storekeeper." This was all very different from the busy world of modern commerce and technology where, as Benjamin Franklin is alleged to have been the first to say, "Time is money." But it did not apply in vast regions of the world when he said it, and it does not do so now.

The idea that coinage was somehow invented to save time does not fit the facts; such a sudden change in established custom would probably have been resented. It would have given rise to suspicion about what the ruler or government was getting out of it. People who had with difficulty been able to acquire little pieces of gold and silver would have thought of little else but possible attempts by authority to deprive them of their savings. This was precisely the fear expressed some 1,600 years later by the ordinary people of India.

Keynes on Hoarding

Then J. M. Keynes advocated the withdrawal of gold coinage to prevent hoarding, which he regarded as wasteful. He believed that the use of gold coins resulted in locking up much wealth in a barren form. I regard this view as fallacious because, as I showed in my *Two Philosophies of Money*,[1] gold hoarding represented a bulwark against the encroachment by governments or rulers on individual freedom. From the point of view of the people of India, the precious metals were the only real money they could trust—as they had rightly trusted them for millennia in the face of successive conquerors and changing political circumstances. Hoarding was, in any case, their only means of personal insurance against uncertainty. In India a reduction of hoarding would probably have come only from an increased sense of social and economic *security* rather than from deliberate attempts to restrict the use of gold. The hoarding of gold simply showed that it was regarded by the people as the best form of *money*. The whole history of coinage and paper money serves as justification of their fears.

---

[1] S. Herbert Frankel, *Two Philosophies of Money: The Conflict of Trust and Authority* (New York: St. Martin's Press, 1978), pp. 58–59.

John Law

One has only to remind oneself of the extraordinary changes in John Law's opinions in the eighteenth century as he pursued his ill-fated monetary policies, which were so arrestingly described by Charles Rist. First Law proclaimed the convertibility of bank notes into metal. Then he suspended the convertibility of the bank notes in order to issue more of them. To conceal their depreciation, he prohibited public possession of gold and silver, ordered searches in homes, seizure of silver in banks and its replacement by paper money, and so on. All this was justified on the grounds that money is made to circulate and, if one hoards it, the king (nowadays the state) has the right to confiscate it. In the words of Law, quoted by Rist:

> And, in truth, the king alone should possess species today, because he is the only debtor in silver, and private individuals owe each other only bank notes. The Bank, in relation to finances, is the heart of the realm, where all the money must return in order to begin again its circulation. Those who wish to amass it or to withhold it are like parts or extremities of the human body that would stop, as it flows, the blood that feeds and restores them. These parts would soon destroy the agent of life in the heart, in all the other parts of the body, and finally in themselves. Money is yours only by the right that you may have recognized by the government certificate to be used to satisfy your needs and your desires. Outside of this right its use belongs to your fellow citizens, and you may not deprive them of it without committing a public injustice and a crime against the state.[2]

As Rist pointed out, what Law really intends to condemn is hoarding —still the nightmare today of the partisans of paper money, for whom money is made only to circulate, not to serve as a store of value.

Let me return to the question of coinage. What is significant is not why in antiquity people did without coinage for so long but why and how it developed at all.[3] For coinage, as I have emphasized, involves trust in authority, and this, to say the least, was usually at a discount.

---

[2] Charles Rist, *The Triumph of Gold*, trans. Philip Cortney (New York: Philosophical Library, 1961), p. 118.

[3] Rudolf Kaulla, *Rechtsstaat und Währung* (Stuttgart and Cologne: W. Kohlhammer, 1949).

Lydian Gold

The origin of coinage seems to have been accidental. It probably arose because gold production in the great kingdom of Lydia occurred in a peculiar form. C. H. V. Sutherland, for many years keeper of coins at the Ashmolean Museum, Oxford, in his fascinating and authoritative work *Gold: Its Beauty, Power and Allure,*[4] pointed out that its source, the most famous in the East Greek world of Asia Minor coastlands, was the River Pactolus, which rolled down great quantities of gold dust from Mount Tomolus in the Anatolian highlands. It cut through and washed away the whole matrix of gold-bearing quartz. The kingdom of Lydia, with its famed king Croesus, had as its center the city of Sardis, which became the heart of one of the earliest "world" money economies. Lydia was really founded on this gold, which procured economic expansion along the Asia Minor littoral. Ultimately, under Croesus, Lydia was associated with the world's first true coinage, which consisted of pure gold coins and pure silver coins. The road to this achievement provides the first documented case study of the emergence of monetary trust.

What was of crucial importance was that Lydian gold was found only as a natural gold-silver alloy, formed as the metallic dust rolled down in the River Pactolus and washed out of it. The ancients did not know how to separate the gold from the silver. The alloy, in which the proportions of gold and silver varied considerably, was known as "white gold" or "electron." Electron was to all intents and purposes found only in Lydia, where it occurred in such relatively large quantities that it came to occupy the dominant position as a means of payment.

But the trading nations outside Lydia's borders were accustomed to using pure gold and silver by weight. Lydian merchants had therefore to exchange their pieces of electron for such gold and silver. As long as Lydia's foreign trade was small, this inconvenience was unavoidable. The Lydian economy as it developed, however, assumed a very important place in the new "money economy" of Asia Minor. It attracted trade from the whole of the Greek world. It therefore became crucial to assure foreign holders of electron that it could indeed be used at all times, without loss, as a means of payment in Lydia.

---

[4] C. H. V. Sutherland, *Gold: Its Beauty, Power and Allure* (London: Thames and Hudson, 1959), p. 65.

15

Stamped Money. Since it was impossible for an individual trader to establish the proportion of gold and silver in each electron piece, the use of electron entailed much uncertainty. The name "electron" could cover large variations in the actual gold content. To establish *trust and confidence* outside Lydia, the expedient was adopted of stamping each piece of electron to identify it as a reliable means of payment in Lydia itself.

This development was in the interests not only of Lydia and its traders but also of the king, who was the biggest trader and the biggest owner of electron gold. It thus came about that the marks of identification on electron pieces to show their origin came in the first instance from the king's treasury. In any case, the use of a stamp to distinguish and identify special metal pieces or bars had long been customary. The Phoenician traders had in this way identified the origin of their metal bars and so provided at least a moral confirmation of their quality.

When the Lydians now put a stamp of origin on their oval electron pieces, or pellets, which in themselves were not well suited for currency, the object was to cause them to be regarded as such: as being as trustworthy as pure gold and silver. There was no state guarantee of their value. Because their origin was certified as Lydian, however, it could be assumed by foreign traders that they would always be accepted in payment for Lydian goods, especially by the king's treasury, which had stamped them.

It is important to note that what was new was not that the stamp guaranteed the material value of the stamped money as really equal to the nominal value but only that the minting authority or treasury would in fact accept it *as if* its metal content corresponded to its nominal value—even if, as was most likely, it did not. These stamped electron pieces were therefore something essentially different from unstamped electron metal. Their nominal value had a protected purchasing power independent of any variation in their real metal content.

Legal Tender. The demand for the stamped pieces naturally grew at the expense of the unstamped ones. In their historical development, we are confronted with one of the earliest examples of a variation between the nominal value of legal tender, used as a means of payment and as a discharge of debts, and the real value of its metallic content. It is an early illustration that every kind of money presupposed the development of public confidence. Every kind of money, including metallic money, rests in part on faith. That was precisely expressed by the succinct inscription on Maltese coins: *"Non aes sed* *fides"*—not by iron but by faith. In it we see the age-old conflict between authority based on power and authority based on trust. It is a conflict between two conceptions: the first, that money is created by the state, which declares not only what shall be its name but what shall correspond to that name; and the second, that money is neither the creation nor the creature of the state but rests on and reflects the promise and performance of society.

Fall of the Electron. This second conception therefore clearly embraces something much more than the technique of regulating and checking the weight and fineness of unstamped money or of the excellence of the coins that later replaced it. The extra ingredient, without which even the most superlative coin could not completely fulfill its function, is public trust and faith in it. The history of money is in a sense but the story of the recurrent failure to maintain that trust and faith, of which the subsequent history of electron currency is perhaps the first recorded example.

It is noteworthy that the value of the electron was not the consequence of any state edict decreeing that the nominal value of the stamped metal pieces would always correspond to their real value. What happened was nothing but the evolution of custom. The agents of the king's treasury accepted payments of taxes, purchased goods and services, and repaid debts in coined money.

In time, however, the history of electron currency ran true to the experience of all later history. The demand for stamped metal grew to such an extent that the minting authorities could exact a seignorage by reducing the weight and fineness of the coins in relation to the nominal value.

The city-states and later other trading nations were soon tumbling over themselves to exploit this new source of profit. Resultant uncertainty about the value of the electron currency finally led King Croesus to issue coins of pure gold and pure silver. By the end of the fourth century B.C., the electron had fallen into disuse almost everywhere; yet even the pure gold and silver coins finally proved no protection for society whenever their debasement seemed useful to the fiscal authorities. Eventually, in both foreign and domestic wholesale trading, there was a return to the old custom of paying by weight in unstamped metal. Truly there is nothing new under the sun: as I write this, many companies and private individuals find it desirable to hold part of their cash balances in gold bullion because they can find no other currency in the world that appears to be as safe.

Falsification of Money

Apparently at no time did governments claim a *right* to determine the value of money or define what should answer as money to the current money of account. Mostly they simply regarded the right as an obvious emanation of their power; they made no moral claim for it or for the constitutionality of its exercise. The repeated abuse of trust in the coinage of the realm proves both the powerlessness of governments to ensure the circulation of a means of payment of stable value and their guile, as when they issued underweight or false coins in a devious manner that covered up their inferiority.

Why should they have done so if they had the power to make money whatever they thought fit, as convinced nominalists like Knapp and Keynes claimed? If the state had the right to declare by a stroke of the pen what was and what was not money, governments would not have needed to resort to guile. They could, in full view of the public, have issued coins or credit instruments or acknowledgments of debt made of any available cheap material and subject only to their decree. The later Roman rulers would not have had to act like any petty swindler by issuing worthless lead coins with a thin coating of gold so as to make the public believe that they were real gold coins, had not the public thought that the worth of the coin depended on its metal content and not merely on the will of the state.

In my view the history of coinage, as later also of paper money, does not support the nominalist view that the state claimed or could claim to be the *fons et origo* of money in the interests of society as a whole. On the contrary, it issued currency in its own interests, claiming that its currency could be trusted—all too often in the knowledge that it could not.

Governments had so often misused their power that it was forgotten, as Carl Menger pointed out long ago (see *Two Philosophies of Money*),[5] that a coin is nothing but a piece of metal, only the fineness and full weight of which are guaranteed by the mint. That government had treated money *as if* it were merely the product of the *convenience* of men and particularly of their legislatures simply multiplied errors about its nature. The repeated debasements by the masters of the mints, by causing the weight of the bullion and the weight of the coins to become different, led to money's being misunderstood. It came to be wrongly regarded as a special measure of exchange value that could be determined or fixed by the state.

---

[5] Frankel, *Two Philosophies*, pp. 33–34.

Against this fallacious view, Menger argued that money was best thought of as the unintended result, the unplanned outcome, of the specifically *individual* efforts of members of society. Lack of space prevents me from following further the story of monetary falsifications. Only in seventeenth-century England did the view prevail that the profit to the treasury from the debasement of the coinage was far outweighed by the loss to the economy.

Seventeenth-Century Developments

The same century witnessed the development of those methods of private and public finance on which the military and economic power of the modern national state was based—that is, credit. It was at this time that the banks of Venice, Amsterdam, and Hamburg were founded. Their primary function was to provide a stable and uniform money of account for international trade—a novel *private* initiative in mobilizing commercial and monetary trust. What these banks did was to assess the value of the many varieties of gold and silver coin that circulated in Europe and buy them from traders by paying for them with *credits* reckoned in their new money of account, called bank money.

At the end of the century, a new development took place that was to prove of signal importance. In 1689 England joined with Holland in the coalition against Louis XIV. In the war that followed, it became necessary to supplement the financial resources of Amsterdam, and in 1694 an entirely new form of credit institution was created to provide money for the government. The money was to be subscribed to a new bank, which was to lend it to the government. That bank was the Bank of England; the modern era of state credit and of paper money had begun. It is astonishing that the belief persists, after nearly three centuries of experience to the contrary, that the value of paper money rests on the power of the governments that directly or indirectly issue it.

Paper Money and Debt

The confusion was often compounded by a misunderstanding of the role of paper money in the discharge of debt. Writing before J. M. Keynes's main works appeared, for example, R. G. Hawtrey had argued in a classic book[6] that the value of paper money is ultimately

---

[6] R. G. Hawtrey, *Currency and Credit* (London: Longmans, Green, 1919).

derived solely from its power of discharging debts; because the purchase of commodities creates a debt, debts have value in the sense that one debt can be exchanged for another or set off against it.

The ownership of a debt thus confers on the creditor general purchasing power; and since persons will always prefer to keep a portion of their wealth in an undifferentiated, unspent form—an option that can be exercised later—there is a demand for credit or purchasing power *as such* that is satisfied by the existence of the unspent margin. It is the demand that determines the value of debts, and the value of paper money is derived from its interchangeability with debts. Hawtrey went even further, asserting that gold itself derived much of its value from its convertibility into credit. It was a standard only a degree less artificial than paper money because its value resulted in part from its legal or conventional characteristic of discharging debts. It differed, however, from paper money because it had some value other than as currency and because its value as currency was recognized across national frontiers.

But who and what are really involved in this power of discharging debts? Clearly a debt cannot be discharged in the abstract merely by creating another debt. It can only be finally discharged by something of value or by canceling or erasing it. When the state makes a bank note inconvertible or issues paper money, it transforms a right to convert the notes or paper money into gold or silver into the right to convert it only into goods or services quoted or priced in the money of account, that is, into dollars or francs or pounds sterling. As Professor M. Allais has rightly pointed out:

> It is essential to understand well . . . that in any kind of economy, *the unit of account cannot exist without a definition that relates it to reality* and that we shall call "the condition of reference." At each moment this definition consists necessarily in determining the nominal price of an "item of reference," constituted by a commodity or a group of commodities. This fixing, though arbitrary as well as *conventional*, is nevertheless indispensable; without it the unit of account would be but a word and would be void of meaning. The conception of a unit of account abstractly defined, independent of any relation with economic reality, would, in fact, be as absurd as establishing as a unit of length an ideal length which one would consider sufficiently defined by calling it meter, without establishing it in a determined object.[7]

---

[7] Quoted by Rist, *Triumph of Gold*, pp. 162–63.

Confusion Compounded

Keynes did not obviate the confusion in this matter. In *A Treatise on Money*, he defined money of account as that in which "Debts and Prices and General Purchasing Power are *expressed*" and as coming into existence along with debts, "which are contracts for deferred payments and Price-Lists, which are offers of contracts for sale or purchase." Money itself he defined as "that by the delivery of which debt-contracts and price-contracts are *discharged*" and "in which a store of General Purchasing Power is *held*." In his view money *derived* its character from its relationship to the money of account in which the debts and prices must first have been expressed. He wrote:

> the money-of-account is the *description* or title and the money is the *thing* which answers to the description. Now if the same thing always answered to the same description, the distinction would have no practical interest. But if the thing can change, whilst the description remains the same, then the distinction can be highly significant. The difference is like that between the King of England (whoever he may be) and King George. A contract to pay ten years hence a weight of gold equal to the weight of the King of England is not the same thing as a contract to pay a weight of gold equal to the weight of the individual who is now King George. It is for the State to declare, when the time comes, who the King of England is.[8]

There follows what is the nub of the issue with which I am here concerned:

> Now by the mention of contracts and offers, we have intro-duced Law or Custom, by which they are enforceable; that is to say, we have introduced the State or the Community. Furthermore it is a peculiar characteristic of money contracts that it is the State or Community not only which enforces delivery, but also which decides what it is that must be delivered as a lawful or customary discharge of a contract which has been concluded in terms of the money-of-account. The State, therefore, comes in first of all as the authority of law which enforces the payment of the thing which cor-responds to the name or description in the contract. But it comes in doubly when, in addition, it claims the right to

---

[8] John Maynard Keynes, *A Treatise on Money*, I (London: Macmillan, 1935), pp. 3–4.

determine and declare *what thing* corresponds to the name, and to vary its declaration from time to time—when, that is to say, it claims the right to re-edit the dictionary. This right is claimed by all modern States and has been so claimed for some four thousand years at least. It is when this stage in the evolution of Money has been reached that Knapp's Chartalism—the doctrine that money is peculiarly a creation of the State—is fully realised.[9]

It is significant and in my view unwarranted that Keynes in this passage used the terms "State" and "Community" interchangeably. He continued:

Thus the Age of Money had succeeded to the Age of Barter as soon as men had adopted a money-of-account. And the Age of Chartalist or State Money was reached when the State claimed the right to declare what thing should answer as money to the current money-of-account—when it claimed the right not only to enforce the dictionary but also to write the dictionary.[10]

Boast of Queen Elizabeth I

Apart from the logical confusion involved in this alleged claim by the state to have the right to declare what thing should answer to the money of account, the claim has little if any basis in historical fact. It is likely that Keynes derived the analogy of the difference between the symbolic king of England and a *particular* king from Hawtrey, who in *Currency and Credit*[11] wrote: "Just as loyalty to the *de facto* monarch, even though a usurper, was recognised as innocent by the law of treason, so with lapse of time a monetary standard, in its origin an immoral debasement, might become entitled to recognition." He referred to the boast of Queen Elizabeth I: *"moneta in justum valorem redacta"* (money has been brought back to its just value). This boast the great prime minister Peel had quoted with approval, in the debates of 1819 in the British Parliament on whether Britain should go back to the gold standard at the parity existing *before* the Napoleonic War. Hawtrey commented that Queen Elizabeth had not in fact gone back to the standard that existed in 1543 but had coined a troy pound into sixty shillings instead of forty-five.

---

[9] Ibid., p. 4.

[10] Ibid., pp. 4–5.

[11] Hawtrey, *Currency and Credit*, p. 369.

What I wish to stress, however, is that Hawtrey missed the important point: that in so doing she did not presume to decide what should be the *value* of the pound but declared its value to be *what through the market society had already brought about*. To illustrate what I mean, let me relate a personal experience.

An Ill-Fated Scheme

In the 1950s the British government entered upon an ill-fated scheme to produce peanuts (groundnuts) on a vast scale in Kongwa, a district of Tanganyika (now Tanzania) in Central Africa. The acreage covered by the project was so vast that even someone standing on a high hill could not see the boundaries of the virgin land that had been cleared for this colossal experiment. After millions of pounds of the British taxpayers' money had been wasted, a working party, of which I was a member, was sent out to assess what should next be done.

When I arrived at the scene, I was met at the airport at Kongwa, the center of the operation, by the chairman of the working party. An enterprising but somewhat inexperienced newspaper reporter accosted him and asked point-blank, "Is it true that your working party has really come out from Britain to write off the groundnut scheme and not give it further help?" To which the chairman replied laconically, "Don't be a damn fool, young man—it has written itself off already!"

A Hollow Claim

The alleged claim of the state to have the right to declare what should answer as money is not only morally questionable; it is a hollow claim. In the last resort, money is only that which will *in fact* discharge debt—not that which merely declares that the debt has been discharged or promises to discharge it. This is illustrated by the present tendency of industry, commerce, and finance throughout the free world to safeguard themselves against depreciation by making contracts and expressing debts in forms that wholly or in part endeavor to circumvent or supplant the use of suspect national currencies or national moneys of account.

The important contemporary issues thus raised can be illustrated by further consideration of the classical theory of money, from which Keynes dissented. Hawtrey was also critical of it in theory, but by no means so emphatically when it came to policy recommendations, which he formulated much more cautiously than did Keynes. The reason for this is revealing and still important. It bears directly on the apparently almost insoluble problems that face all policy makers. What was at issue was the fundamental postulate underlying the classical theory of currency, namely, that any two things exchanged must each have *value*: if goods or services are sold for money, the money must have value; if they are sold for credit, the credit must have value. It follows that credits can be used as a substitute for money because and only because they give a title to money:

> that a piece of paper which purports to confer this right, but does not in fact do so, has in reality no value; it is a promise to pay, which is not kept. Paper money which is not convertible into coin is a sham, a fraud. He who sells goods for paper money sells something for nothing; likewise he who sells them for a credit payable only in paper money. Coin only differs from bullion in that its weight and fineness are certified. If it does not contain the prescribed amount of fine metal the certificate is an imposture.[12]

In Hawtrey's opinion the consequence of this *"severe uncompromising doctrine"* (emphasis added) was to obscure the true nature of a money of account because, if a credit has no meaning other than an obligation to pay so much gold, there is no room for the whole conception of a unit for the measurement of debts as distinguished from a unit for the measurement of gold. He regarded the neglect of the distinction as innocuous as long as debts were in fact payable in gold but not when the monetary system became deranged and debts were no longer payable in gold. It was on just such occasions that currency theories, "which may usually be left to the care of economists, gain practical and political importance."

Thus, for example, in the debates of 1811 in the British House of Commons on the classic Bullion Committee Report (which recommended a return to the old gold parity of the English pound), the opponents of the report argued that it was based on purely abstract theories. To these critics Canning replied:

> The admonition to beware of abstract theories comes from whom? From the inventors and champions of "abstract currency"—from those who, after exhausting every attempt to find an earthly substitute for the legal and ancient standard of our money, have divested the pound sterling of all the properties of matter, and pursued it under the name of "ideal unit" into the regions of non-entity and nonsense. I

[12] Ibid., p. 364.

24

contend that a certain specified weight of gold or silver, of a certain fineness, is the only definition of a pound sterling which an Englishman, desirous of conforming to the laws of his country, is bound to regard or understand.[13]

Critique of Classical Theory

This in Hawtrey's view was the essence of the classical theory. It held the word "pound" to mean or imply a certain definitive quantity of gold; a pound was nothing else than the *promise* to pay to the holder that definitive quantity. He contended that the supporters of the classical doctrine failed to grasp the meaning of a money of account, which was something distinct from legal tender. To arrive at that conception, one had to realize that an undischarged debt due from a solvent debtor was purchasing power from the standpoint of the creditor. Since there was a demand for purchasing power *as such*, it had a price like anything else.

The money of account, argued Hawtrey, was the unit in which not only debts but also prices were expressed. So long as the quantity of purchasing power is not unduly increased, prices are not disturbed, and the value of the monetary unit of account remains steady. Since this could not be relied upon, the *expedient* had been adopted of fixing the price of the commodity; gold had been given its coinage price, and every debtor could be required to pay in gold at that price. This could not possibly mean, however, that the monetary unit of account had no *meaning* other than the precise weight of gold or silver it represented at the coinage price. He pointed out that, at the very time of this historic currency debate, the value of the pound in which debts and prices were actually reckoned had depreciated by 20 percent.

A Categorical Imperative

The argument for a fixed, unalterable parity of gold was not that no other monetary system was possible. Rather it was that, since this monetary system actually existed, an engagement to pay a pound must be interpreted in its light. *To discharge it in any other way than by paying the stipulated quantity of gold would be a breach of faith.* The real foundation of the classical theory was the belief that it is not enough to prove that it is invariably *expedient* to maintain a metallic standard but that a departure from it must be shown to

---

[13] Ibid., p. 366.

be actually *dishonest*. The system must be securely founded on a categorical imperative.

Hawtrey recognized that the categorical imperative, a universally binding law—as in Kant's ethical system—did not necessarily preclude *any* change of monetary standard. What he criticized was the idea that such a change involved a *moral* issue. It was his belief (a belief that has become commonplace) that an alteration of the monetary standard was a question of expediency—of policy—that had nothing to do with the keeping of promises or other moral considerations.

Nominalism

This was basically also Keynes's view. He derived it from Georg Friedrich Knapp, who had asserted that the monetary unit is purely nominal. The franc, the dollar, and the florin do not connote a fixed weight of metal. They are abstract units. In this conception, once a money has been established, it can be changed only on the basis of an acceptance of the nominal character of the monetary unit and the recognition that only the state can change the means of payment, while the relative magnitude of different debts remains the same.

Whatever else one may think of such definitions of money, one thing is certain: they do not rest on any particular moral conception. They are merely formal and juridical or, as Knapp said, historical.

The nominalist approach and the fallacious conclusions to which it led also permeate the work of Keynes and his followers. There is the same appeal to history. Because the monetary standard, when it was linked to the precious metals, varied and was unjust to creditors or debtors, to admit a value criterion in the form of a metal content as the basis of the monetary standard is really to abandon any moral or ethical element. There is also Hawtrey's argument:

> If a purchaser contracts to pay money neither party to the agreement considers in what medium the debt will be payable. The medium of payment and consequently the value of the debt will be settled by the law of the land. The medium of payment in fact is not part of the contract. And this is true as much of a promise to pay as of an obligation to pay. If payment were desired in any particular medium, this would be expressly stipulated.[14]

Therefore, it is concluded, the moral objections of the classical school to inconvertible paper money fall to the ground.

---

[14] Ibid., p. 370.

But do they? I contend not. In my view the contrary is true. Historical experience has shown again and again that when the medium of payment fails to meet the expectations of debtors or creditors, contracts will be made in *other* monetary forms or by barter agreements to circumvent the "nominal" money that the state endeavors to impose. *Alternatively, certain kinds of monetary contracts will not be made at all;* the currency risks involved become too great as trust in the "legal" money of account is undermined. That is why, with high rates of inflation, long-term money contracts are curtailed in favor of those that involve only short-term currency risks.

To abandon moral considerations is to appeal to *expediency* and to be exposed to the risks of abuse that it involves. This Hawtrey finally recognized. He continued:

> If a paper issue is so regulated that the foreign exchanges are kept near par, and that the purchasing power of the monetary unit in terms of commodities does not vary unduly, then the advantages of a sound currency system have been obtained. But unless there is some generally recognised international standard of value these conditions may be unattainable and may not even be consistent with one another.[15]

This is just a way, however, of shifting the burden of moral, political, and economic decision making to those countries prepared to assume the maintenance of the international standard. In the absence of agreement to adhere to a metallic standard, who will determine what the standard shall be? Who will be responsible for its management? Who will guarantee trust in it? It is surely worth pondering, when we survey the present impasse in monetary affairs, Robert Giffen's warning over eighty years ago:

> No change in a monetary standard, if it is a tolerably good one, ought to be proposed or considered unless upon grounds of overwhelming necessity. For a good money is so very difficult a thing to get, and Governments, when they meddle with money, are so apt to make blunders (and have, in fact, made such blunders without end in the past . . .) that a nation which has a good money should beware of its being tampered with, and especially should beware of any change in the foundation—the standard for money. Locke, and

---

[15] Ibid.

other older economists, went further, and maintained that a change of standard should *never* be made, because every change involves injustice. But without going so far as this, we may recognise that there are various practical reasons for not changing lightly or readily—that is, for not changing for any other reasons than those of overwhelming necessity. These considerations apply especially to the standard for money in a country like England, where the standard is the foundation of a fabric of credit, whose extension and delicacy make the slightest jar apt to produce the most formidable effects.[16]

Giffen was quite clear about what he meant by a monetary standard. There was to be no tampering with it or mincing of words about it. To obtain a good monetary standard, the thing that was the standard should itself be the medium in which payments were made; alternatively, the medium should consist of currency readily convertible, on the basis of an index number, into the thing that was the standard. A tabular standard could never be so regarded.

Monetary experience since World War I reveals that the maintenance of *any* monetary standard involves the willingness and ability of society to take *responsibility for it, to be accountable for its operation, and to fashion and maintain the institutions to support it.*

This is a difficult task; it involves the art of government, which, it has truly been said, is of all tasks the most difficult. But it will not do to conclude that, because it has always been difficult to establish or maintain a trustworthy money, the attempt to do so should be abandoned. It is possible neither to avoid the moral and political issues involved, since both action and inaction have consequences, nor to regard them as the prerogative only of the state or of government.

---

[16] Robert Giffen, "Fancy Monetary Standards," *Economic Journal,* vol. 2 (1892), p. 465.

3

John Locke on Money

The Significance of Money

It was John Locke (1632–1704), "the great Locke" as Keynes called him, who was the first to set out the basic moral issues raised by money. He was one of the first writers to explain how money helps to transform subsistence economies by enlarging the market, increasing productivity, and making saving and capital accumulation possible—all of which were so conspicuously lacking in societies in the "state of nature." As an example of the change brought about by the introduction of money, he chose the primitive unexplored America of his time; today he could point to large regions in Africa, Asia, and South America in which local currencies, with a very restricted role, predominate.

It was money, Locke emphasized, that released man from this narrow dependence on nature. It replaced the utter dependence on nature by a new dependence, a dependence on other individuals and on society, which would protect individuals from one another. Unexplored America in its pristine state was for Locke and his contemporaries the prime example of man in a state of nature; an early stage of man could be seen and studied there.

> Thus in the beginning all the World was *America*, and more so than that is now; for no such thing as *Money* was any where known. Find out something that hath the *Use and*

A part of this chapter is being published under the title "Monetary Freedom: John Locke and the Keynesians," in Gerhard Merk, ed., *Acta Monetaria Yearbook of Monetary System and Money Policy* (Frankfurt am Main: Fritz Knapp, 1980), vol. 4.

Value of Money amongst his Neighbours, you shall see the same Man will begin presently to *enlarge* his *Possessions*.[1]

It was necessary, argued Locke, to overcome the wastefulness and destruction by spoilage that limited production in the original state of nature. Then a man would find it reasonable to produce more than was necessary for his own family's immediate wants, more than they could consume before it spoiled. For this reason, money was invented. In Locke's view, it came into existence naturally. Men first bartered perishable foods for more durable foods, such as nuts; later they traded goods for a piece of metal whose color pleased them.

And thus *came in the use of Money*, some lasting thing that Men might keep without spoiling, and that by mutual consent Men would take in exchange for the truly useful, but perishable Supports of Life.[2]

Extension of the Money Economy

My own experiences bear out the keenness of Locke's powers of observation. I have witnessed the amazing consequences—in the space of only some twenty-five years—of the extension of the money economy in Kenya after individuals were permitted to own, buy, and sell land and thus, for the first time, to accumulate capital.

These legislative changes took place in no small measure as a result of the work of the East African Royal Commission 1953–1955, on which I served. They had not been made before owing to the opposition, or fear of it, of the majority of the population, who were still wedded to the wasteful old system of communal landownership. This was based on an age-old fallacy that Locke criticized—namely, if a man encloses land and claims to own it so as to cultivate it, he necessarily injures society. In vast regions of Africa and elsewhere, the fructifying effects of free monetary transactions have not been introduced because of prohibitions by law or custom. Under some authoritarian regimes, such as that in Tanzania, progress in the extension of a previously existing free money economy has actually been deliberately arrested.

Protection of Individual Freedom

A second strand in Locke's thought, which has, unfortunately, been largely neglected, is his treatment of money as an essential element

---

[1] John Locke, *Two Treatises of Government*, ed. Peter Laslett (Cambridge: Cambridge University Press, 1960), Second Treatise, para. 49, p. 319.

[2] Ibid., para. 47, pp. 318–19.

in the protection of the free personality of the individual. For Locke the right to possess, use, and store up money is fundamental. Like the ownership of property, it is not conferred on the individual by society, but rather civil society has been established to protect this right. This view is important for a proper understanding of our present monetary difficulties.

Two well-known dangers in considering Locke's ideas should be emphasized: to read more into Locke's written words than they will bear; and to ignore or overlook what he did write or to assume that he could not have meant what he had written. C. B. Macpherson falls victim to the first danger.[3] He ascribes to Locke, as John Dunn has shown,[4] a concern with an ideological debate about the respective virtues of capitalism and communism that is more relevant to our time than to that of Locke. Many modern economists have fallen victim to the second danger. They have been more concerned to discover how far Locke understood the theoretical analysis of economic problems that now interest us but were not being discussed in modern terminology when he wrote. The fact is that Locke's concerns were not those now in fashion. They were less time-bound and more fundamental.

Moral Principles

Locke, it must be remembered, was a man of affairs and a public servant acquainted with the workings of government, the City of London, the Bank of England, and the British Treasury. Above all, of course, he was a great moral and political philosopher solely concerned with the freedom of the individual and all it involved for his happiness—in the world to come, be it noted, as well as in this world. He was therefore concerned not only with the freedom of the individual to acquire property but also with the duty to use it in accordance with moral principles. He was conscious both of the individual's rights and of his duties and obligations—among which the duty of practical charity was not the least important.

As John Dunn has stressed, for Locke, social and therefore market values are to a considerable extent conventional, but

> beneath the flexible and diversified structure of social convention, there remains the rigid and unitary order of nature

---

[3] C. B. Macpherson, *The Political Theory of Possessive Individualism: Hobbes to Locke* (Oxford: Oxford University Press, Oxford Paper Backs, 1962).

[4] John Dunn, *The Political Thought of John Locke* (Cambridge: Cambridge University Press, 1969).

and its demands have none of the permissive delicacy of human complaisance, for they are the demands of God. All men have a duty to preserve their fellow man to the best of their ability. It is the duty of charity. Where a seller exploits a particular market so far as to endanger the preservation of the buyers he offends against the common rule of charity as a man.[5]

Locke wrote at the commencement of a new era of individual economic self-expression. By contrast, we have in this century become accustomed to the denigration of the economic role of the free individual.

The difference between the social background at the time Locke was writing and our current attitudes can be illustrated by the following passage from Saul Bellow's Nobel Lecture. In it he contrasted Joseph Conrad's views of life and art with those of writers "for whom the Conradian novel—all novels of that sort—are gone forever. Finished." For them *"there are no characters; you find in such books not individuals but—well, entities"* [emphasis added]. Bellow quotes one of these writers, Robbe-Grillet: "The present period is rather one of *administrative numbers*. The world's destiny has ceased, for us, to be identified with the rise and fall of certain men of certain families." The title of Robbe-Grillet's essay is "On Several Obsolete Notions." Criticizing the essay in defense of individuality, Bellow continued:

> I myself am tired of obsolete notions. . . . But I never tire of reading the master novelists. And what is one to do about the characters in their books? Is it necessary to discontinue the investigation of character? Can anything so vivid in them now be utterly dead? Can it be that human beings are at a dead end? Is individuality really so dependent on historical and cultural conditions? Can we accept the account of those conditions we are so "authoritatively" given?[6]

Defense of Individuality. For Locke the defense of individuality was paramount and money an essential constituent of that defense. It is therefore not astonishing to find that his treatment of the importance of money far transcends the petty calculations of the misers or spendthrifts of this world, governments included. For him the essence

---

[5] John Dunn, "Justice and the Interpretation of Locke's Political Theory," *Political Studies*, vol. 16 (1968), pp. 73–74.

[6] Saul Bellow, "There Is Much More to Us . . ." *Dialogue*, vol. 10, no. 3 (1977), pp. 61–67.

of money was trust between individuals: trust at home and trust abroad based on the making and keeping of promises and contracts.

He perceived, as few had done before him, that the evolution of money was also the evolution of social relations. The fact that his reflections on money are not technically as advanced as ours pales into insignificance beside the wide sweep of his treatment of money's role in the defense of freedom. As Peter Laslett wrote:

> Locke's psychological insight may be imperfect, his logic often odd, his general standpoint ungrateful to our generation and not easily understood even within his own personal historical context. . . . But after he had written and what he had written had had its enormous impact on the European mind, it was no longer possible to believe that politics went forward in a moral sphere in which the good man was the good citizen. Citizenship was now a specific duty, a personal challenge in a world where every individual either recognized his responsibility for every other, or disobeyed his conscience. Political duties have not changed since then.[7]

Money and Consent

It was Locke's view that the right of the individual to use money (by which, of course, he meant gold and silver) is a fundamental right that precedes any assumed or real compact that brought men into civil society:

> it is plain, that Men have agreed to disproportionate and unequal Possession of the Earth, they having *by a tacit and voluntary consent* found out a way, how a man may fairly possess more land than he himself can use the product of, by receiving in exchange for the overplus, Gold and Silver, which may be hoarded up without injury to any one, these metalls not spoiling or decaying in the hands of the possessor. This partage of things, in an inequality of private possessions, men have made practicable *out of the bounds of Societie, and without compact*, only by putting a value on gold and silver and *tacitly agreeing in the use of Money* [emphasis added].[8]

In this connection I refer to John Dunn's important conclusion as to what John Locke meant by consent:

---

[7] Peter Laslett, Introduction to Locke, *Two Treatises*, p. 120.

[8] Locke, *Two Treatises*, Second Treatise, para. 50, p. 320.

In the *Two Treatises*, men are said to consent to many different states of affairs and to do so in many different ways. Consent is said to be present at the inception of legitimate policies. It occurs on every occasion at which an individual by explicit or implicit choice becomes a member of a legitimate political community. It appears whenever a community chooses its representatives in the manner to which it has previously consented and whenever these representatives vote. It is responsible for the rise of a money economy and it is an attribute of every subsequent monetary transaction.[9]

Dunn also stresses that for Locke "money *was* an institution, a product of human contrivance and convention, not of natural necessity." He quotes a passage from the Italian translation of Locke's monetary writings: "It should not be understood that our author (Locke) meant to speak of a convention in the real acceptance of the term, but rather of a custom (or usage) in which men have agreed among themselves unconsciously and tacitly, for their own convenience and advantage."[10]

The Law of Nature

As Dunn has explained in the article already mentioned, Locke's *Two Treatises of Government* was not written as a set of instructions on how to establish political societies *ab initio*. Rather, his aim was to draw implications from conceptions underlying a previously existing and constitutionally sound political community. Some form of consent in a settled political society is necessary to protect the "State all Men are naturally in" (that is, before they have by agreement entered into society). This "State all Men are in" is "a *State of perfect Freedom* to order their Actions, and dispose of their Possessions, and Persons as they think fit, within the bounds of the Law of Nature, without asking leave or depending upon the Will of any other Man [emphasis added]."[11]

In Dunn's view, Locke held that if a man cannot be said to have been consulted, he has been coerced. Dunn concludes:

No express limits are implied logically in the conception of laws which the sovereign may pass to regulate property.

---

[9] John Dunn, "Consent in the Political Theory of John Locke," *Historical Journal*, vol. 10, no. 2 (1967), p. 160.

[10] Dunn, *Political Thought*, p. 118, n. 2. Translated for me from the medieval Italian by Professor C. Grayson of Oxford.

[11] Locke, *Two Treatises*, Second Treatise, para. 2–6, p. 287.

But all such laws are subject to invalidation by the higher principle of the law of nature. A law which had the effect of removing a man's property without his consent would be in breach of the law of nature.[12]

Dunn points out that in general this could happen only if a law in breach of the law of nature and without a man's consent did not meet the criteria of positive legality in society. Locke's position, however, is precisely that

> There may be no internal legal grounds which make invalid the [formally legal] arbitrary and malicious confiscation of property; but higher law considerations provide no support for such unjust enactments. . . . To suppose that there are [positive] legal reasons why a formally valid law can be voided for moral impropriety is a logical error. To suppose that all formally valid laws are morally obligatory is a moral error. Neither error is made by Locke.[13]

Money Prior to Society

Macpherson has remarked that, while the introduction of money is by consent, it is not the same consent as that which brings man into civil society. The consent to money is independent of and *prior* to the consent of civil society.

For Locke the right to possess and use money is man's natural right just as it is his natural right "to preserve his Property, that is, his Life, Liberty and Estate."[14] He meant by property "that Property which Men have in their Persons as well as Goods."[15] Locke's emphasis on the individual's right to possess money rests on the contention that men are naturally capable of "other Promises and Compacts" than the compact assumed to have established civil society: "For Truth and keeping of Faith belongs to Men, as Men, and not as Members of Society."[16]

As Raymond Polin has expressed it:

> the compact through which the people bind themselves to a body politic as a government . . . is of a moral nature: it constitutes the famous trust, which would not be compre-

---

[12] Dunn, "Consent," p. 164.

[13] Ibid., pp. 164–65.

[14] Locke, *Two Treatises*, Second Treatise, para. 87, p. 341.

[15] Ibid., para. 173, p. 401.

[16] Ibid., para. 14, p. 295.

hensible if it did not bind by their moral commitments, beings similarly capable of intelligence and freedom, the people and their rulers. *A trust as such binds beings capable of committing themselves, capable of promising—in a word capable of freedom* [emphasis added].[17]

On Promising

Hannah Arendt, writing of the influence of social contract theories on American experience in similar terms, expressed their essence:

In distinction to strength, which is the gift and the possession of every man in his isolation against all other men, power comes into being only if and when men join themselves together for the purpose of action, and it will disappear when, for whatever reason, they disperse and desert one another. Hence, binding and promising, combining and covenanting are the means by which power is kept in existence; where and when men succeed in keeping intact the power which sprang up between them during the course of any particular act or deed, they are already in the process of founding, of constituting a stable worldly structure to house, as it were, their combined power of action. There is an element of the world-building capacity of man in the human faculty of making and keeping promises. Just as promises and agreements deal with the future and provide stability in the ocean of future uncertainty where the unpredictable may break in from all sides, so the constituting, founding, and world-building capacities of man concern always not so much ourselves and our own time on earth as our "successors," and "posterities." . . . The act of foundation by virtue of the making and the keeping of promises . . . in the realm of politics may well be the highest human faculty.[18]

Locke's Ethical View of Man

It has been argued that "to postulate, as Locke does, that men are by nature rational enough—both in the sense of seeing their own interest and in the sense of acknowledging moral obligation—to make the more difficult agreement to enter civil society by handing over

---

[17] Raymond Polin, "John Locke's Conception of Freedom," in John W. Yolton, ed., *Problems and Perspectives* (Cambridge: Cambridge University Press, 1969), p. 13.
[18] Hannah Arendt, *On Revolution* (London: Faber and Faber, 1963), pp. 174–75.

power to the majority in it is to presume that men are also rational enough to make the less difficult agreements required to enter into commerce."[19] Of course, men are here considered in the abstract; the argument is not an inference from history or primitive society. Men are thus, abstractly speaking, assumed to have a commercial economy quite independent of their formal civil society. This has been interpreted as meaning that "neither money nor contracts owe their validity to the state; they are an emanation of the natural purposes of men and owe their validity to man's natural reason. It is, on this view, the postulated *moral* reasonableness of men by nature, not the authority of a government, that establishes the conventional value of money and the obligation of commercial contracts."[20]

This interpretation, although it stresses that in Locke's view money is not the creation of the state, does not fully reflect the significance of Locke's argument. It endeavors to express his views in purely hedonistic terms. It suggests that we must hold that there is no virtue in Lockean civil society but only the brutish pursuit of self-interest. As against this view, Donald J. Devine argues that

> Locke's political philosophy simply starts with his ethical view of man, morally equal because created by God, each having an obligation to choose the good. Each, accordingly, is created free but he is expected by God to use that freedom responsibly by following God's law so that he will merit eternal reward.

This view of freedom makes only the individual ultimately valuable; since all institutions were created by individuals, such institutions are inferior to them. To obtain agreement in society, Locke assumes

> that people must have some acquaintance and friendship together and some *trust* in one another; that this *trust* will then permit them to make a common agreement as to the type of regime all "think good," and that what they think good must be defined by the value principles they hold which specify the good.[21]

Society and the State

Locke's views on money rest on his distinction between society—as the repository of virtue—and the state. As Devine has pointed out:

---

[19] Macpherson, *Political Theory*, p. 210.

[20] Ibid.

[21] Donald J. Devine, "John Locke: His Harmony between Liberty and Virtue," *Modern Age*, vol. 22, no. 3 (Summer 1978), pp. 250–52.

The Lockean society which has a government, therefore, is not one which is value-free or, without virtue. . . . Rather Lockean society assumes values and is distinguished from others only in the locus of its values and virtue, which are placed in individuals within society as opposed to the state. This distinction between society as the repository of virtue and the state as only a *means* to regulate coercion, indeed, is what defines Lockean society. Hence, in this type of regime, the government is given the very limited, though important function of only defining and regulating coercion. Otherwise, it is to allow virtue to develop spontaneously in society as the result of free decisions of individuals, since society is the higher repository of virtue, honor, esteem, reverence, etc. which are the *ends* of life.

In other words, "Government's only morality is to conduct its own affairs morally and otherwise virtue rests in society."[22] Thus, given that the government ensures peace and controls coercion, individual liberty and virtue are not in fundamental conflict but are perceived to be in harmony, provided that the people have "some trust in one another."[23] The only real protection of the basic rights of life, liberty, and property (including money) is trust that the authorities will not abuse them or that, if they do, the majority will correct the abuse. "It is a measure of the importance of values in the Lockean regime that it assumes that the majority will act virtuously."[24]

The Lockean view rests ultimately on a particular conception of the relation between individuals and society. It is a view that generally reflects the attitude toward the role of money that was later dominant, particularly in the nineteenth century.

As I have shown in *Two Philosophies of Money*, the most important element of that view was that society is nothing but the combined expression, the general name, for the interrelations between individuals. Society is not something additional to or apart from them. It is an error to regard money as something additional to that for which it is used. It cannot be regarded as being, as it were, an empire of its own. Indeed, the common practice of ascribing to the state (or government) powers in monetary affairs that it does not possess is based on this error. Money is nothing apart from the objects, in the form of goods or services, on which it is spent. It reflects their free objective valuation by individuals through the process of exchange,

---

[22] Ibid., p. 252.
[23] Ibid.
[24] Ibid.

38

without which money does not function fully. Whenever the freedom to express values in money is abrogated, the function of money is correspondingly curtailed; it loses its raison d'être as the medium for and symbol of the *contractual* relation between individuals, whether made in the past or the present or covering the future. There is an intimate relationship between money and freedom, between the keeping of promises and the certainty of contracts, between social function and the rules of law. Indeed the power of the state to create or control money is limited by the fact that, the more money it endeavors to compel people to accept in defiance of individual market preferences, the less trust and confidence money will command.

The Dissent from Contractual Theories

In the light of this analysis, the question that demands attention is why the contractual concept of liberty, and correspondingly of money, has not been more fully accepted. A whole generation has followed Keynes in dissenting from it. A clue to the answer was given in 1900 by Georg Simmel in his classic *The Philosophy of Money.*[25] I did not perceive the full significance of this clue when I wrote *Two Philosophies of Money*, in which I was concerned to stress the importance Simmel attached to money for the defense of individual freedom. For him money was freedom's guarantee: money illustrated the far-reaching and complex nature of the concept of freedom. At first glance freedom seems to possess a merely negative character. It has meaning only in contrast to a form of bondage; it is always freedom from something. It expresses the absence of obstacles.

This is also the essence of the Lockean, the Victorian, and all other contractual theories of money. They are not more generally accepted because freedom would be without meaning and value if its advancement did not also imply some gain in another direction: in power or possessions. In other words, freedom *from* something necessarily implies freedom *to* do or freedom *for* something else.

The Disillusion with Money

But *what* else? In the answer to that question lies the common fear of responsibility and also the fear, the dissatisfaction, the disillusion with money itself. Simmel illustrates the phenomenon as follows:

---

[25] Georg Simmel, *The Philosophy of Money*, trans. Tom Bottomore and David Frisby (London: Routledge and Kegan Paul, 1978).

In political life, wherever a party demands or attains freedom the issue is not at all one of freedom as such, but those positive gains, increases and spreading of power from which the party was previously excluded. The importance of the "freedom" which the French Revolution gave to the Third Estate was that a Fourth Estate was in the making which could now be required to work "freely" for that estate. The freedom of the Church means the direct extension of its sphere of influence, for example, that with reference to its "freedom of instruction" the State permits its citizens to be exposed to and influenced by the Church's suggestions. The liberation of the peasant-serfs all over Europe was followed up by endeavours to make the peasant the owner of his plot of land—just like the ancient Jewish regulations, which requested that the indebted slave had to be liberated after a certain number of years, while adding that he should be handed over some property, preferably that which he formerly owned. Wherever the purely negative sense of freedom operates, freedom is considered to be incomplete and degrading.[26]

One can easily multiply these instances. A striking example of the disastrous failure to follow the granting of negative freedom with positive freedom is the liberation of the slaves in the southern United States. Many slaves suffered great hardship because of the failure to provide land or employment opportunities for them after they had been freed. Simmel gives the example of Prussian cottagers whose lands were located outside the community farmland, where the various holdings lay in mixed strips that could only be cultivated in accordance with common rules. The cottager was freed from these rules and therefore had much more *negative* freedom. Because he no longer had the *positive* freedom to participate in the making of communal decisions regarding the fields, however, he remained in an inferior position with very little social prestige, even if he had considerable property.

The Limitations on Freedom

If we analyze the events by which freedom is gained, Simmel points out, we always notice, alongside the formal and pure concept of freedom, a real (or substantive) content. This, however, by giving freedom a *positive* significance, also *limits* it by laying down a direc-

---

[26] Ibid., pp. 400–401.

tive as to what has to be done with it. In money transactions, the negative factor of liberation from former constraints predominates over all other relations. If somebody sells his property for cash, he is really free, in the negative sense, from all but very minimum constraints on his future course of action. Simmel notes, however, the danger in which a peasant finds himself when he sells his land. He is "liberated" by the cash he receives, but the freedom he has thus gained places him in a dilemma—the dilemma of all human freedom: he has gained freedom only *from* something, not freedom *for* something. *Apparently he gained freedom to do anything,* but since this freedom was purely negative, he was left without any definite goal. He was brought face to face with the need and the responsibility for making new choices. He had lost his custom-bound social and economic security.

In a passage that is perhaps even more relevant now than when it was written, Simmel pointed out that such freedom favors that emptiness and instability that permit one to give full rein to every accidental, whimsical, or tempting impulse. Such freedom is comparable to the fate of the insecure person who has forsworn his gods. His new "freedom" provides only the opportunity to make an idol out of any fleeting value. The tradesman who urgently sells a burdensome business at any cost meets with the same fate. When finally, cash in hand, he is really "free," he often experiences the boredom, lack of purpose in life, and inner restlessness typical of the rentier, which drive him to the oddest and most contradictory attempts to keep busy in order to give a substantive content to his "freedom." That also is the experience of the official who is eager to retire on his pension so as to lead a "free" life. Amid the torments and anxieties of the world, the state of repose often appears to us to be the absolute ideal until we learn by experience that peace from specific things is valuable or even bearable only if it is, at the same time, peace to engage in specific things.

Even more significant for an understanding of dissatisfaction with the free money economy is Simmel's analysis of the relation of money to the objects bought with it. In earlier times the personal labor that went into producing or decorating things gave them an individual stamp. Things were a kind of extension of the ego, an expression of personality long treasured as an individual bond between them and the owner. Today we have more freedom but are unable to enjoy it properly; money makes it possible for us to buy ourselves not only out of bonds with others but even out of bonds with our own possessions. We develop a rootless search for ever *new* things because money is our only nexus with them. Money's abstract power to command *anything* ultimately seems to command *nothing*.

The Disillusion with the Money Economy

The importance of these reflections lies in the light they throw on the growing dissatisfaction with the free contractual money economy. They also highlight the psychological resistance to the Lockean concept of contractual monetary freedom. Such freedom involves the ever-growing responsibilities of personal choice. It leads also to the apparent need by governments and individuals to acquire money for the power it *seems* to confer automatically, yet without any certainty or guarantee that it will do so.

As a consequence, increasing numbers of individuals seek to escape from the negative freedom money involves—freedom from the restraint of others—into a new type of freedom. Modern writers have called this the substitution for the negative *freedom from* of the positive *freedom to*, that is, to be told, led, persuaded, or coerced to do something for or with others or to leave it to them to do, so that the individual is no longer responsible for choosing and deciding. This surrender to new purposes can be ennobling and constructive, exhilarating, and apparently liberating. Yet, as history has demonstrated, it can also be degrading, debilitating, and harmful. "Freedom to" is limiting because it always rules out, to some degree, the free choice of other alternatives.

Money illustrates this dilemma most forcefully. The very fact that it is without content until it has been put to specific use makes it appear *as if* it were available for *any* use at *any* time. It therefore seems to be the ideal agent for furthering *any* purpose. This is a delusion that makes it appear *as if* the problem of choice had been eliminated. Actually the transfer of money simply means that it has passed to others who now have to make the choice of what to do with it; the problem of choosing correctly has not been solved.

Money as a Partisan Issue

The shifting of responsibility is reflected, as Simmel showed, in the origin of the word "partisan." The word originally referred to a moneylender who was *party* to a loan to the French crown. Later, owing to the resulting mutual interests of bankers and the minister of finance, the term acquired the meaning of an *unconditional supporter*. When the ill-fated assignats (paper currency) were first introduced, it was officially emphasized that, wherever the currency existed, its reliability *ought* to be regarded as a public duty. This was an attempt to enlist the support both of those *politically interested* in the measures being taken by the state and of those *creditors* (for example, bondholders) who financed the measures and would therefore be concerned about their success.

The parallel with current everyday experience of the insatiable demands of modern governments for money, whether raised by taxation or by loans, for every conceivable purpose, is obvious. Whether governments, rather than private individuals, should exercise this money power has become a *partisan* issue resting on ideologies about what should be done rather than on whether it can or will be done economically.

Herein lies the root of the inflation of our time. Money issues— money being thought of in the abstract—have become partisan political issues, not issues of individual accountability or responsibility for success or failure. But the problems of success or failure cannot be thus conveniently pushed into the background. Ultimately, those who have surrendered their decision-making powers to others in the pursuit of ideological causes, however good in themselves, cannot escape the consequences. Yet this obvious fact continues to be overlooked or ignored.

Money in the Abstract

Let me give two examples of the consequences of considering money in abstract terms. The first is the now common practice among neo-Keynesian writers of assuming that capital not supplied through the market by private saving and investment can simply be replaced by state expenditures financed by loans or taxation. If mortgage finance for private construction falls, it is suggested, governments (local or central) need only step into the breach. The fallacy in such thinking is that the operations of government do not by any means necessarily correspond to those of individuals in the free market and are not subject to the market's constraints and penalties when they fail to meet the real demands of consumers. The fallacy arises from considering the powers of money in abstract terms and forgetting the required actions of individuals who alone can bring money to life.

My second example is an account of a tragic occurrence. Recently a young man in the United States created a vast industrial concern following upon a new invention. His success was not only the result of the invention; it was due largely to his personal recruitment of each of his sales managers from among people with whom he had previously worked. He continued to keep their complete trust through *personal* contact with them in national marketing of the product. Unfortunately he was killed in an airplane accident. At a subsequent meeting of the shareholders, the acting chairman announced that the late chairman's life had been insured for $5 million, which now accrued to the company. He added that so far no one could be found to replace the chairman; he could only hope that the company could continue *somehow* to be as successful as before. So much for the abstract powers of the insurance money that accrued to the company.

It was the same tendency to confuse the theoretical powers of money with the reality of the constantly changing and developing contractual relations of individuals that formed the basis of Joseph A. Schumpeter's theory of economic development. He repeatedly stressed the point, nowadays so often overlooked, that the essential problem of a free market economy and of capital investment in it lies in the power of any individual with knowledge and enterprise to dissolve outworn combinations of economic resources and substitute new ones in accordance with consumer demands, in other words, the freedom to translate abstract money and credit into actual new situations for the production of goods and services.

That, of course, was the reason Locke was so concerned with freedom in the contractual society. It is a freedom that neo-Keynesians have both wittingly and unwittingly derided or ignored in attempts to express and control the activities of society in terms of assumed monetary aggregates, which are necessarily estimated abstractions from past and present reality. In so doing they have overlooked the problem that production must meet *real* demands and aspirations. When it fails to do so—and the failure is reflected in the present world inflation—those who have surrendered their freedom from restraint to rigid institutional authorities to act on their behalf become impoverished and disillusioned and eventually turn to gods other than those that have failed them.

4
Corruption of the Money Economy

Encroachments of Political Authority

In the preceding chapter, I indicated some of the reasons for current fears and apprehensions about the contractual money economy based on free individual responsibility. To grasp the nature of the monetary predicament now facing the free world, let us look again at the Lockean defense of money. Locke was, as we have seen, concerned with finding a basis for protecting individual rights "held under positive law against the arbitrary encroachments of political authority."[1] That defense of money rested on what would now be called the need to ensure negative freedom—freedom for the individual to use money or to keep it as he saw fit, secure from the arbitrary action of governments.

It is worth reminding ourselves that these formulations were not made or conceived in the abstract. They were the result of a long debate concerning social and political action. It was Locke's aim to defy the absolutist state, once the ally of freedom but now its suppressor.

The Emergence of Economic Freedom. Before the sixteenth century, a vast network of private trade, banking, and finance had slowly developed that crisscrossed Europe from Italy to the Low Countries, France, and England. It was based, despite regional and local obstacles, on a freedom of economic traffic that had not existed since Roman times. It was eventually dominated by great commercial and financial enterprises, such as those of the Bardi, Peruzzi, Medici, and Fugger

---

[1] John Dunn, "Justice and the Interpretation of Locke's Political Thought," *Political Studies*, vol. 16 (February 1968), p. 68.

families. Hand in hand with this development went the growth of national monarchical states. Their growth could, however, be regarded as progressive because they brought about a degree of political stability that was exceptional in relation to the anarchy and disorganization of feudal society. But, as Louis M. Hacker reminds us in *The Triumph of American Capitalism,*[2] the absolute royal power eventually sought to dig itself in behind the barriers of privilege. With the growing cost of dynastic wars and the extravagance at royal courts, the merchant class began to feel the weight of the royal exactions: the judiciary began to operate in star-chamber proceedings, the tax collector and farmer began to be more oppressive, and the royal monopolies began to cut into free commercial and productive enterprise.

The Bureaucracy of Absolutism

In England and France, the monarchy strengthened the numbers and position of the new court nobility, which became the bureaucracy of absolutism. Its members controlled the national churches, sat on the bench, officered the armies and navies, and received the most lucrative monopolies. Directly and indirectly, they were turned loose on the people for spoliation. The sixteenth- and seventeenth-century absolutist monarchies of England and France built up great companies of personal retainers that, in effect, became the controllers of the regimes—not unlike the arbitrary bureaucracy of today's authoritarian states. By the seventeenth century in England and the eighteenth in France, it seemed to the middle classes that their chances for growth would forever remain stunted unless monarchical privilege was restricted. A government of laws had to be established to protect liberty and property against arbitrary procedures. This was accomplished in the Puritan Revolution of the seventeenth century and the French Revolution of the eighteenth century.

These events are relevant for us even now because we witness in them the attempt, finally abortive, by the crown to entrench itself permanently as the head of a corporate economy in which the individual's rights were completely subordinated to those of the state.

Archbishop Laud, the great spokesman for Stuart absolutism, made a statement in a sermon he delivered in 1621 that typified this totalitarian ideology:

---

[2] Louis M. Hacker, *The Triumph of American Capitalism* (New York: Columbia University Press, 1956).

If any man be so addicted to his private interest that he neglects the common State, he is void of the sense of piety, and wishes peace and happiness for himself in vain. For whoever he be, he must live in the body of the commonwealth and in the body of the church.[3]

How sharply the conception of the role of the state had changed after the revolution is shown by the contrast between Archbishop Laud's statement and John Locke's summing-up only fifty years later in *A Letter Concerning Toleration*:

The Commonwealth seems to me to be a Society of Men constituted only for the procuring and preserving and advancing of their own civil interest. Civil interest I call Life, Liberty, Inviolability of Body, and the possession of outward things such as Money, Lands, Houses, Furniture, and the Like.[4]

Modern "Economic Man"

As a result of the Civil War and the "Glorious Revolution" in England, modern "economic man" had emerged. A century later he was intellectually enthroned by Adam Smith; finally he was enshrined in the American Constitution.

The new spirit exalted labor as the chief moral aim of life. It supported the idea of the self-regulation of industry by free competition based on the untrammeled evolution of the individual.

The resulting liberal state was thus something very new, and the contractual view of money to which it gave rise, it must be emphasized, arose very late in the history of monetary development. The political conceptions on which it rests were, until modern times, strongly condemned and were in practice resisted. They are still resisted.

The Classical View

From the time of Plato and Aristotle, money had always been suspect. It was thought of not as protecting or extending the personality of the individual but as corrupting him—compromising what constituted his freedom as a citizen. The essence of that freedom was seen as the exercise of the *active* virtue of citizenship. This classical view was revived in the Florentine Republic. It can be epitomized as the right

---

[3] Ibid., p. 69.
[4] Ibid., p. 81.

and duty of the free and independent individual, as a citizen, "to join in the determination of priorities." This was not "freedom from" being but "freedom to" be a participant in the affairs of the polity.

In this view of liberty, to be barred from the decision-making process is a kind of servitude. Civil virtue is attained through the citizen's political activity for the *common* good, not through his private actions for his *own* good. For the citizen of the ancient polis the question was not, What are or should be the limits on the governing authority? (the Lockean question), but the very different question, Who (what sort of person) should govern?[5] That person must above all be independent, secure in his independence, and incorruptible in it. His authority and autonomy must rest on his ownership of land and his willingness to take up arms to defend both it and the republic of which he was privileged to be a citizen.

The Corruption of Commerce. The ethos of the ancient city-states was essentially narrow. Money and commerce were regarded as potentially corrupting because those who were producers of goods for exchange became aware of new values and therefore likely to endanger those values prescribed by law, custom, or authority. They were, no doubt, thought of as corrupting for much the same reasons that now cause the Soviet Union to prohibit free individual exchange, free markets, and free commercial intercourse with foreigners or foreign countries. The opening of the mind to new thoughts and experiences is regarded as dangerous. So also in the ancient world it was held that if citizens were permitted to trade outside the city walls, they would enter into human relations and develop codes of human values over which the republic would have only a contingent authority.

That is why Plato found it necessary to prohibit commerce outside the city and leave the socialization of the personality entirely to music and other modes of education controlled by the guardians. Nowadays dictators use the mass media to do the same. In the eighteenth century, Montesquieu summed up the austere classical view in his remark that commerce is the source of all social values save one . . . but that one, the *virtue politique*, is the one that makes man *zōon politikon*, by nature a citizen,

> and consequently human; and there is a radical disjunction
> between the two categories of value. Commerce, which
> makes men cultured, entails luxury, which makes them

---

[5] J. H. Hexter, *On Historians* (London: Collins, 1979), p. 302.

corrupt; there is no economic law which sets limits to the growth of luxury, and virtue is to be preserved only by the discipline of the republic, educating men in frugality.[6]

Pocock has reminded us that for Machiavelli the concept of arms expressed both the citizens' total devotion to the republic and the notion that the world outside the republic was too harsh and dangerous to permit citizens to profess ideas of any universal humanity toward it. The survival of the republic was constantly threatened by fortune, by the flux of things in time, and by history, the enemy of human fulfillment.

The Unresolved Issue. From the middle of the seventeenth to the end of the eighteenth century, there was continuing tension between this Machiavellian view and the other view that arose out of the commercial and foreign policies of the emerging modern states. As we shall see, that tension remains unresolved in the free world of today. It lies at the root of the current monetary malaise.

What gave rise to it in English and later in American political debates in the seventeenth and eighteenth centuries was the problem of how the citizen could retain his virtue, in accordance with the classical view, in a new world of growing wealth based not on land-ownership but on mobile property. These debates played a significant role in the drafting of the American Constitution, which in a sense can be seen, as Pocock has suggested, as the last act of the civic humanist tradition and Machiavellian thought concerning the *zōon politikon*. The American Founders can be looked upon as having occupied a "Machiavellian moment" in history, by which Pocock means a crisis in the relation between personality and society, virtue and corruption.

The still unresolved issue arose from the eighteenth century's realization that the ideal of personality, which in the past had been seen as "sustained by property" (that is, "natural" and "real" property in the form of inheritable land), might be undermined by monetization, by increasing dependence on credit and on public debt, which rested unavoidably on mere hope and fantasy. As a result, crises of confidence and uncertainty would increasingly take the place of the stability conferred by the ownership of land and all that went with it. Trust in the unpredictable vagaries of state policies was seen

---

[6] J. G. A. Pocock, *The Machiavellian Moment: Florentine Political Thought and the Atlantic Republican Tradition* (Princeton: Princeton University Press, 1975), p. 492.

to be replacing trust in the promises of economically independent individuals.

In the past the function of property—particularly real, inheritable, and "natural" property in land—was

> to affirm and maintain the reality of personal autonomy, liberty, and virtue . . . it must if possible display a reality (one is tempted to say a realty) capable of spanning the generations and permitting the living to succeed the dead in a real and natural order. Inheritance, therefore, appeared more than ever before the mode of economic transmission proper to a society's existence in time. Land and inheritance remained essential to virtue, and virtue to the ego's reality in its own sight; there is an element of existential fear about the dread of corruption so prominent in eighteenth-century social values. For the ideal of personality-sustaining property was no sooner formulated than it was seen to be threatened. . . . Forms of property were seen to arise which conveyed the notion of *inherent dependence: salaried office, reliance on private or political patronage, on public credit.* For these the appropriate term in the republican lexicon was corruption—the substitution of private dependencies for public authority—and the threat to individual integrity and self-knowledge which corruption had always implied was reinforced by the rise of forms of property seeming to rest on fantasy and false consciousness. Once property was seen to have a *symbolic value, expressed in coin or in credit*, the foundations of personality themselves appeared imaginary or at best consensual: the individual could exist, even in his own sight, only at the fluctuating value imposed upon him by his fellows, and these evaluations, though constant and public, were too irrationally performed to be seen as acts of political decision or virtue [emphasis added].[7]

The Dangers of Dependence

These new forms of property were regarded as bringing about an inescapable dependence on what we would now call the bureaucracy, on private pressure groups, and on government expenditure—all inescapably corrupt or corrupting of the individual's free decision-making role. Corrupting, let me repeat, because in the traditional view:

> The polity must be a perfect partnership of all citizens and all values since, if it was less, a part would be ruling in the

---

[7] Ibid., pp. 463–64.

name of the whole . . . and moving towards despotism and the corruption of its own values. . . . The citizen must be a perfect citizen, since if he was less, he prevented the polity from attaining perfection and tempted his fellows, who did for him what he should have done for himself, to injustice and corruption. To become the dependent of another was as great a crime as to reduce another to dependence on oneself.[8]

A Benign View of Credit

This is why the eighteenth-century debate on the nature of credit was waged so long and so fiercely. Gradually, however, there evolved what we may designate a "benign" view of the credit economy that was to overcome or suppress these fears. This view was in a sense a rationalization. It began to be argued that, since the expansion of credit was obviously necessary for trading and power-seeking nations, what was really important was that credit should be properly managed; its well-known irrationalities and uncertainties, which had been compared to those of fortune, could be held in check by a trustworthy government and appropriate private conduct:

> To the extent to which the credit economy could be convincingly presented as based on the exchange of real goods and the perception of real values, it could be divorced from the threat of false consciousness and endowed with concepts of the public good and personal virtue. In what scholars have called a "Protestant ethic" of frugality, self-denial, and reinvestment, trading society could even be permitted its own version of that classical virtue which consisted in placing the common good (in this case the circulation of trade) above one's personal profit.[9]

Indeed, credit was depicted as a *public* being, which can exist only where men have confidence in one another and in the kingdom. In the words of Daniel Defoe, writing in 1710:

> *Credit* is not dependent on the Person of the Sovereign, upon a Ministry, or upon this or that Management; but upon the Honour of the Public Administration in *General*, and the Justice of *Parliaments in Particular*, in keeping whole the Interest of those that have ventured their Estates upon the Public Faith—Nor Must any *Intervention of Parties* be of Notice in this Case—For if one Party being uppermost shall

---

[8] Ibid., p. 75.

[9] Ibid., p. 464.

refuse to make good the Deficiencies of the Ministry *that went before them*, because another Party then had the Management, *Parliamentary Credit* would not be worth a Farthing. . . . *Credit* is too wary, too Coy a Lady to stay with any People upon . . . mean Conditions; if you will entertain this Virgin, you must act upon the nice Principles of Honour, and Justice; you must preserve Sacred all the Foundations, and build regular Structures upon them; you must answer all Demands, with a respect to the Solemnity, and Value of the Engagement; with respect to Justice, and Honour; and without any respect to Parties—If this is not observ'd, Credit will not come; No, tho' the Queen should call; tho' the Parliament should call, or tho' the whole Nation should call.[10]

New Confidence in the Currency

It is beyond the scope of this study to examine the legal and administrative measures that put into practice in Great Britain the nineteenth-century policies based on such ideas. Suffice it to say that they were consciously aimed at creating a state of confidence in the currency and overcoming economic crises that might disrupt the beneficent industrial, financial, and commercial effects of a trustworthy credit economy based on honest money. The way out of the dilemma was thought to lie in the assumed inherent dynamism of the monetary free-exchange economy. The promise of economic progress held out by it was regarded as the guarantee both of the value of money and of the political and economic independence of the individual. Moreover, the dynamism of the market economy could be regarded as firmly entrenched as a result of the general belief in the overriding necessity to fashion such monetary policies as would further the market's efficiency and would maintain faith in the money economy on which it was based.

Bagehot on Credit

It was not just a flourish of the pen that caused Walter Bagehot to write: "Credit is a power which may grow, but cannot be constructed. Those who live under a great and firm system of credit must consider that if they break up that one they will never see another, for it will take years upon years to make a successor to it." For Bagehot a

---

[10] Daniel Defoe, quoted by Pocock, *Machiavellian Moment*, p. 455.

money market such as "Lombard Street," which was then equivalent to the "Wall Street" of today, was "a luxury which no country has ever enjoyed with even comparable equality before." By this he meant that it was a heritage from the past—a result of the growth of personal character and of the reputation for reliability. In short, it was based on trust. For him credit in business was like loyalty in government.

It was true, he argued, that a theorist could easily map out a scheme of government that dispensed with Queen Victoria, because the House of Commons was the real sovereign; but for practical purposes, he thought, such arguments were not even worth examining. If those millions who loyally obeyed Queen Victoria without doubt and without reasoning were to begin to argue, it would not be easy to persuade them to obey Queen Victoria or anyone or anything else. Effectual arguments to persuade the people who needed persuasion would be wanting.

The same was true of the immense system of credit founded on the Bank of England:

> The English people, and foreigners too, *trust it implicitly.* Every banker knows that if he has to *prove* that he is worthy of credit, however good may be his arguments, in fact his credit is gone: but *what we have requires no proof. The whole rests on* an instinctive confidence generated by use and years.[11]

But the dilemma remained, in spite of a hundred years of vast economic progress in the countries that secured and maintained the operation of the free market and monetary policies appropriate to it.

The Ghost in the Machine

The ghost in the machine that affrighted the eighteenth century had not been exorcised: what still haunted the individual in the modern economic system, even though that system appeared to sweep everything before it, was that he felt himself becoming less, not more, secure. Like so much else, the money economy forced him into increasing dependence on the success with which irrational, unpredictable fears and hopes and the fluctuations of mass optimism or pessimism could be contained.

As an individual he *should* have felt secure; according to Locke

---

[11] Walter Bagehot, *Lombard Street: A Description of the Money Market* (London: H. S. King, 1873), p. 68.

and his successors, the inviolability and stability of monied property guaranteed security. The illusion of that security persisted until the outbreak of World War I, as readers of Galsworthy's *Forsyte Saga* will recall. Galsworthy depicted the property owners as naturally, and without hesitation, investing in gilt-edged British Consols (Consolidated Exchequer Bonds), which were considered so riskless that the British Treasury did not even have to fix a date for their redemption. The property owners thought that the value of the bonds, like the value of money, would remain unimpaired forever.

The Threat to Security

But the general sense of security, so taken for granted, was nonetheless artificial, fragile, imaginary, or, as money was frequently called in the seventeenth century, *fantastical*—a word, now obsolete, that the *Oxford English Dictionary* defines as then meaning "arbitrarily devised, unreal."

A careful student of Locke would have been aware of the lurking danger to this security. Locke's main thesis concerning consent was that only through society could the natural rights of man be secured—even the free contractual use and value of money were in this sense "fantastical," that is, contrived by society, *which always had to defend them*. Locke's aboriginal social contract, Hannah Arendt has argued, has to be understood in the Roman sense of *societas*. It brought about not government but a community, an alliance between all individual members who contract for their government after they have mutually bound themselves by promises.

This is the horizontal version of the social contract. While limiting the power of each individual member, it left intact the power of society. Locke had argued that the power that every individual gave to society when he entered it could never revert to that individual again, as long as the society lasted.

Hannah Arendt has suggested that the signers of the Declaration of Independence were thinking both in this vein and also in terms of the specifically American experience. Seen in this perspective, tacit consent is, she thought, not a fiction but inherent in the human condition. The tacit agreement must, however, be carefully distinguished from consent to specific laws or specific policies. A tacit agreement does not imply consent to statutory laws because in a representative government people have helped to make them. It certainly does not imply automatic consent to the acts of the bureaucracy.

Twentieth-Century Conceptions

The consensual theories that played such a pivotal role in relation to monetary policy in the nineteenth century gave way to quite different conceptions in the twentieth. These were concerned far less, if at all, with the protection of the money of the individual against the arbitrary authority of the state. On the contrary, they regarded the idea of providing a secure social framework for individual decision making and risk bearing in a stable money environment as of relatively little importance.

The new conceptions rested on the thesis that what mattered was economic *development* and that this was part of a political and social *process*, which could be expressed in abstract aggregate money terms in the form of statistical models. In this process the economic role of the individual entrepreneur was belittled because, it was argued, he really knew no better than anybody else what should be done. He certainly knew less than anybody who was charged with determining the rate at which the social and economic growth process appropriate to the aggregate monetary targets should be fixed or what fiscal or monetary actions were appropriate to those targets.

Experts, those able to exercise what Keynes always called public wisdom, would necessarily have to undertake the supervision of the development process. In this process money would play a social role in which its moral significance, as a standard of value or of deferred payments in fulfilling promises or discharging debts, was of little significance. These ideas, which increasingly dominated monetary policy in many countries, first in Great Britain and subsequently in the United States and elsewhere, did not arise accidentally. They were discussed in a considerable specialist literature long before World War I.

The Irrationality of Private Calculation. The basic argument advanced in this literature was that the optimistic belief that somehow *private* monetary calculation could further the general good was irrational. According to this argument, the very idea of the economic rationality of the entrepreneur or businessman was itself irrational. The much-vaunted rationality of business enterprise was simply the exercise of reason in a social setting in which society had so organized the conditions of enterprise that the businessman, in following the profit motive, was able to succeed. He did so not because he necessarily acted rationally in the interests of the whole society but simply because he acted rationally in his *protected* situation. Why, then, should the monetary standard be tailored to the needs of private economic risk bearing?

Keynes was greatly influenced by these views. The whole monetary system, about which he was so ambivalent, sometimes appeared to him to be a contrived system of pretty techniques, made for a nicely regulated market that would give capitalists and businessmen a sense of certainty and security. Keynes even associated their failure directly with money motives and money calculations. To him these were not really scientific because they were based on money-getting aims that were incapable of dealing with uncertainty.

Skepticism about the beneficence of money could hardly have gone further. The consequences of such views are discussed in the next chapter.

5

The International Order

Mercantilism

Every society has to determine how far it will permit individuals to engage in commerce and finance across national frontiers—how far its domestic monetary arrangements will interlock with those existing beyond its borders.

These arrangements may, of course, be developed haphazardly, or they may be imposed upon the society by political or economic circumstances or by other nations. Whatever the case may be, the monetary factors cannot be considered in the abstract or as existing apart from the political and moral beliefs involved. In other words, the problems of monetary policy are but one aspect of the general problems of a nation's "virtue," which, as we have noted, forms part of all its relations with other nations and necessarily includes the willingness of its citizens to defend it by taking up arms against other nations.

The contractual or laissez-faire conception of money was developed when mercantilism was in its heyday, and it is not accidental that Keynes, in *The General Theory of Employment, Interest and Money*,[1] gave renewed attention to its tenets. He realized how closely they coincided with the fundamental monetary issue of our time. He clearly envisaged the possibility of a return to them and, although he espoused some mercantilist views, he also endeavored to find a new way. These endeavors culminated in the ill-fated Bretton Woods agreements, which were intended to overcome narrow national preoccupations. How far Keynes was himself consciously or uncon-

---

[1] John Maynard Keynes, *The General Theory of Employment, Interest and Money* (London: Macmillan, 1936).

sciously influenced by concern for Great Britain's own peculiar situation remains a moot question. The point I am anxious to stress here is that he was one of the few who clearly understood the nature of the modern monetary predicament. Although he could not have hoped finally to find a way of escaping from it, the reasons for his failure require examination.

Mercantilist Nationalism. Keynes recognized that the advantages claimed by the mercantilists, based as they were on protectionist attitudes, were purely *national* advantages not intended to benefit other nations. What has been loosely called the mercantilist system was the reverse of the laissez-faire liberalism that succeeded it. Its outlook was based on the driving idea of enlarging and maintaining state power and resembled that of authoritarian states today. It aimed primarily at enlarging the isolating power of the national state, not at promoting the economic freedom of the individual across national boundaries—that aim characterized the nineteenth century. The mercantilist powers looked upon the regions or countries that they dominated as their economic preserve. The situation of the dependent regions was not unlike that of some countries behind the Iron Curtain today.

Insufficiency of New Investment

Why was Keynes so sympathetic to mercantilism? The answer to that question, I suggest, is to be found in Keynes's view that, when a country is rapidly growing in wealth, its growth is likely to be interrupted *under conditions of laissez faire* because of insufficient inducements to new investment. Such inducements come either from investment at home or from investment abroad; the latter, of course, in mercantilist doctrine, included the accumulation of the precious metals.

Keynes argued that when there is no question of direct investment by or under the aegis of the state or other public authority (that is, when aggregate investment at home and abroad is, under laissez faire, determined solely by the profit motive), home investment will be governed in the long run by the domestic role of the rate of interest, and foreign investment will depend on the size of the favorable balance of trade. In these conditions, he thought it reasonable for the government to be mainly preoccupied with the rate of interest and the balance of foreign trade.

The mercantilists seemed to Keynes realistic in their indifference to the advantages of an international monetary system. He preferred their realism to the confused thinking of the advocates of an international gold standard and laissez faire in international lending. He thought that in an economy on the gold standard, and subject therefore to relatively long-term fixed money contracts, there was no orthodox means available to the authorities to counter unemployment at home.

He wrote:

> Never in history was there a method devised of such efficacy for setting each country's advantage at variance with its neighbours' as the international gold (or, formerly, silver) standard. For it made domestic prosperity directly dependent on a competitive pursuit of markets and a competitive appetite for the precious metals.[2]

It was Keynes's opinion that the opposite held true; what was needed was an autonomous rate of interest unimpeded by international preoccupations. He advocated a national investment program directed toward an optimum level of domestic employment. This would be twice blessed in the sense that it would help "ourselves and our neighbours at the same time" and would permit the simultaneous pursuit of these policies by all countries.

Conflicting Goals

Unfortunately, this approach and the assumption on which it was based did not make clear how the monetary relations of individuals in the free world economy would be affected. This gap in monetary thought and practice remains unfilled.

For over thirty years, we have been witnessing the inefficient and inflationary consequences of neo-Keynesian theories based on the belief that through monetary policy each country can pursue goals that are at *one and the same time* in the supposed *national* interest of each nation and miraculously also in the general international interest of all of them. This, of course, was not at all what the mercantilists were saying or what their policies attempted to translate into practice. They had no illusions about the monetary limits of their powers. They were concerned solely with their *own* national interest as they saw it.

I wish to stress that it is not possible to discover from day to day or from crisis to crisis a monetary policy that will serve to

---

[2] Ibid., p. 349.

harmonize, outside the operations of individuals in a free world market, the conflicting needs or aspirations or whims of every nation-state; nor is it possible to rely on an international bureaucracy to do so. The experts, the politicians, and the people, whether at home or abroad, do not know, nor can they possibly know, what such a policy should be.

Category Mistakes

It should be noted that the interests to be thus harmonized are not, in general, monetary at all. To present them in abstract terms as if they were is to do injustice to the real nature of these problems. It is to make a logical leap from one category of thought to another. Two of Keynes's historical examples illustrate this point.

Spain. Keynes believed that the foreign trade of Spain in the latter part of the fifteenth century and in the sixteenth century was destroyed by the effect on the wage unit of an excess of the precious metals. In fact Spain's foreign trade was destroyed not by the excess of the precious metals but by the rigidity of its outworn social, economic, and financial structure, which prevented it from taking advantage of the new supplies of the precious metals. Indeed, not Spain but the economically vigorous Netherlands made full use of them through progressive new commercial and credit institutions that were the envy of other nations. The Dutch were able to attract from the effete and custom-bound Spaniards all the precious metals they required. We have not far to seek for parallel developments at the present time. We need only contrast the industrial growth of Hong Kong with the relative economic rigidities in Europe and in the United States, not to mention the obstacles to economic change in the so-called Third World countries.

As I write these words, efforts have again become necessary to deal with the inability of many of the Third World countries to pay even the interest on the vast loans they have received from private banking sources and international agencies during the last two or three decades. The economic plight of these countries results in no small measure from the way money was made available to them for "national" purposes. Too little regard was given to the social and economic structures of these countries and to the real demands in domestic and foreign markets to be met if the borrowed money and their own resources were not to be wasted.

Foreign Lending. Keynes was concerned that, from a *national* point of view, foreign lending in Great Britain before World War I had been *excessive*, so that the domestic rate of interest tended to be too high. Both of Keynes's examples contain the same logical error. Keynes backed up his belief that, left to market forces, the domestic rate of interest could not be relied on unaided to stimulate sufficient investment at home. He suggested that the actual experiences of the mercantilists led them to the belief that there had been throughout human history a stronger propensity to save than to invest. The weakness of inducement to invest had been at all times the key to the economic problem.

Significantly, he admitted that risks and hazards of all kinds might formerly have played a larger part in restraining investment—a situation to which, I fear, we may now be returning. But finally, it was that "the desire of the individual to augment his personal wealth by abstaining from consumption has usually been stronger than the inducement to the entrepreneur to augment the national wealth by employing labour on the construction of durable assets."[3]

Universal Dynamic Ideal. In support of this opinion, Keynes[4] also quoted the following passage from Eli F. Heckscher's classic book *Mercantilism.*

> Within the state, mercantilism pursued thoroughgoing dynamic ends. But the important thing is that this was bound up with a static conception of the total economic resources in the world; for this it was that created that fundamental disharmony which sustained the endless commercial wars. . . . This was the tragedy of mercantilism. Both the Middle Ages with their universal static ideal and *laissez-faire* with its universal dynamic ideal avoided this consequence.[5]

Keynes, however, failed to discuss *how* the twentieth century could maintain *its* "universal dynamic ideal." If neither the Middle Ages nor mercantilism could overcome static conceptions and disharmonies, the question was why the twentieth century was clearly also failing to overcome them. In my view the failure arose from the facile belief that the free market did not and could not overcome them—that the

---

[3] Ibid., p. 348.

[4] Ibid.

[5] Eli F. Heckscher, *Mercantilism* (London: George Allen & Unwin, 1935), vol. 2, pp. 25–26.

national states had to shoulder the main burden of economic "development" and "growth" at home and abroad (through international agencies and governments).

Profitability and National Advantage

Let me return to Keynes's contrast between profitability and national advantage. The logical error here lies in moving from a category of thought that expresses "profitability," which can only be discussed in money terms, to a different category of thought—the augmentation of the "national" wealth through the construction of "durable" assets, neither of which can be discussed in terms of profitability or of money.

A similar logical error occurred when, in regard to certain laws that compelled trustees to invest abroad, Keynes argued that "large sums may flow abroad without there having been a *vestige of deliberate calculation on the part of anybody that this is the best way of employing the resources in the national interest*" [emphasis added].[6]

Significantly, however, he did not indicate anywhere how such a calculation could be made. He was, nevertheless, very critical of the criteria of calculation that had led to private investment. To lend vast sums abroad for long periods without any possibility of legal redress if things went wrong, he thought, was crazy—especially when the sums were lent in return for a trifling extra interest.

In adopting this argument, Keynes was shifting the discussion to an entirely different plane. He was no longer discussing the obstacles to the application of those accounting criteria of calculation that are necessarily used by an *investor*. He was throwing those criteria overboard altogether. Keynes asked the reader to consider

> two investments, the one at home and the other abroad, with equal risks of repudiation or confiscation or legislation restricting profit. It is a matter of indifference to the individual investor which he selects. But the nation as a whole retains in the one case the object of the investment and the fruits of it; whilst in the other case both are lost. If a loan to improve a South American capital is repudiated we have nothing. If a . . . housing loan is repudiated, we, as a nation, still have the houses. If the Grand Trunk Railway of Canada fails its shareholders by reason of legal restriction of the rates chargeable or for any other cause, we have nothing. If the

---

[6] Keynes, "Foreign Investment and National Advantage," *The Nation and the Athenaeum* (August 1924), pp. 985–86.

Underground System of London fails its shareholders, Londoners still have their Underground System.[7]

This argument ignored the conceptual basis of nineteenth-century international investment, which, despite frictions and political interferences, assumed that for investment purposes the world economy of the great powers *was one, and should be regarded as one.* In fact, it did function broadly as a unit; an international division of labor and investment did develop that was less influenced by deliberate political and economic barriers than at any time before or after this unique period.

To put the matter differently, Keynes's argument that it was absurd to invest in a Canadian railway, even if the index of profitability indicated that such an investment was more desirable than an investment in the Underground Railway System of London, would itself have been regarded as absurd. At that time the London underground was thought of as serving a metropolis of the world. London, it could have been argued, might not have required an underground system if it had remained the capital of "a little England."

I wish to emphasize again that arguments concerned with the alleged "national advantage or disadvantage" of foreign investment are not based on, and cannot be considered as if they were based on, *investment* criteria. Such arguments involve discussion on two different planes of thought: discussion about the "profitability" of *investment* assumes a common accounting standard or symbolism, whereas discussion about national advantage or disadvantage denies it.

The Wrong Target

Adam Smith, in a well-known passage, warned against confusing the language of trade and the language of national power:

> The sneaking arts of underling tradesmen are thus erected into political maxims for the conduct of a great Empire. . . . By such maxims as these, however, nations have been taught that their interest consisted in beggaring all their neighbours. Each nation has been made to look with an invidious eye upon the prosperity of all the nations with which it trades, and to consider their gain as its own loss. Commerce, which ought naturally to be, among nations as among individuals, a bond of union and friendship, has become the most fertile source of discord and animosity. The capricious

---

[7] Ibid.

ambition of kings and ministers has not, during the present and the preceding century, been more fatal to the repose of Europe, than the impertinent jealousy of merchants and manufacturers.[8]

A whole generation since Keynes has been influenced to train its sights on the wrong target. It has been concerned not with the maintenance of the principles underlying the world economy on which every one of the free nations depends but with the pursuit of their individual *domestic* interests and predilections.

Government Intervention

It is significant that policies have been advocated on the contention that the forces of the free market cannot be relied upon, that national interests necessitate government intervention either directly or through monetary policies. Consequently, the need to strengthen the free world economic order, which the nineteenth century regarded as vital to the interests of all its members, was relegated to the background in the belief that if domestic considerations were regarded as paramount, international harmony would ensue. Unfortunately, this has not proved to be true.

In the nineteenth century the growth of wealth was in large measure due to a unique confidence in the maintenance of international commercial and financial contracts. In this century, however, serious difficulties have been engendered by the opposite psychological attitude—doubt and international distrust. Pessimism about *individual* economic enterprise across national boundaries predominates. It arises from the continuing uncertainties caused by the restrictions, rigidities, and unpredictability of national economic and monetary policies.

A Moment of Balance

Let me here draw attention again to the fact that the pre-1914 world economy, compared with our present state of affairs, represented a moment of balance and harmony between internal and external forces. That state of affairs was brought about by governments in the belief that they were engaged in a contest in which each national government had constantly to adjust its monetary policy to outwit its neighbors.

---

[8] Adam Smith, *An Inquiry into the Nature and Causes of the Wealth of Nations*, bk. IV, chap. III.

Such a belief would have been regarded in the nineteenth century as an extraordinary perversion of mercantilist ideas. It would have been seen as a national struggle for power founded not on gold and silver but on paper and debt intended to camouflage deficits at home and weakness abroad.

On the contrary, the pre-1914 situation was brought about because it was realized that what was at stake was the growth of an expanding world economy. The nineteenth-century international gold standard that characterized that situation was a self-denying act by democracy to curb the power of government so as to ensure monetary trust across national frontiers. It worked better in promoting the growth of the world economy than any other monetary system so far devised. Those who ask whether we can return to it must remember the foundation on which it rested: the willingness of the citizens to accept the restraints and obligations it involved.

The harmony between the international and national monetary order reflected individual freedom and was built on it. It rested on a concept of virtue in society that saw no conflict between the individual's rights and duties at home and abroad.

Even after World War I, the illusion persisted that confidence in the international monetary system could somehow be restored. World War II shattered that hope. Once Humpty Dumpty had had a great fall, nothing could be done to put him together again.

New Orientations

The disintegration of the international monetary system was not just a historical accident. It was in large part the result of a belief that monetary policy should have a new orientation. The spirit that inspired the Federal Reserve Act was very different from the spirit that had brought about nineteenth-century monetary discipline. It was now held that conscious control by the central bank could and should be pursued in relation to overall policy objectives. The new watchword was "stabilization"—not of employment, as after World War II, but of the price level. This assumed that what had to be stabilized was known. Unfortunately, it was not.

Even *if* prices in general could have been held stable, it was not known what effect this would have on *particular* prices or employments or trades or classes *relative* to others. There were also limits within which a single *area* could successfully cut itself adrift from the general monetary current.

The Fundamental Question

There was, however, a far more fundamental question. To this day we have not found an answer to it. Sir Theodore Gregory was one of the first to raise it:

> *Quis custodiet ipsos custodes?* Somewhere power must remain. But is it to be a Government Department, an independent National Bank guided by a directorship of merchants, a Nationalised Central Bank inspired by the Treasury, a quasi-public Corporation guided by Mr. Keynes? *Who* is to take the final responsibility? How is such a body to deal with a constitutional opposition, certain to arise, represented by City Editors, Friendly but Critical Economists, Unfriendly but Critical Business Men? These are the kinds of question which must be faced, boldly, honestly and exhaustively, but they find little mention in the literature of the subject up to the present. A project cannot, of course, be "right in theory" but "impossible in practice." Either the theory has overlooked some of the premises, or the practicians have not understood the theory. And probably both these conditions have helped to popularise the idea of stabilisation to-day.[9]

Noting, perspicaciously, how the "long-term" tendency in the modern world was toward interference on political grounds, Gregory asked how the central bank could be safeguarded against class bias or subservience to the financial needs of government. The moral that he drew was that it is undesirable to exaggerate the *plasticity* of the modern economic system and its responsiveness to the dictates of central banks and bankers in general. It was not his intention to suggest that *nothing* could be done, and certainly not that whatever was done could just be left to the central banks. His incontrovertible conclusion was that if stabilization was ever to be attained, it could only be

> because not only the Governors of Central Banks—sitting, like the modern generals, considerably behind the firing line—are aware of, and convinced by, the trend of economic theory, but because the army of industry also knows what the battle is about and has been trained to rise above its momentary weaknesses and temptations in order to achieve victory in the interests of human welfare.[10]

---

[9] T. E. Gregory, "Central Bank Policy," *Manchester Statistical Society* (December 1926), p. 44.
[10] Ibid., p. 54.

The Burden of Citizenship

Few would deny that to exercise the privileges and shoulder the burdens of citizenship, in monetary as in other affairs, has become more onerous and difficult. The citizen desirous of acting virtuously has a new power with which to contend. The extent of bureaucracy has grown beyond recognition, not only within each country but beyond each country's borders, in the form of international agencies that often are as much a law unto themselves as their national opposite numbers.

James M. Buchanan has pointed out that modern man, in the struggle to escape from the tangled web of bureaucracy (that great Leviathan of our time), can rely only on himself or on others like him. "When we speak of controlling Leviathan we should be referring to controlling self-government, not some instrument manipulated by the decisions of others than ourselves. Widespread acknowledgement of this simple truth might work wonders."[11]

The monetary predicament of the free world can be dealt with by none other than its citizens. If they attempt to do so, can they afford to overlook the classical idea of virtue: the need to control the passions, to moderate envy, greed, lust for power, and love of ease at the expense of others and of freedom itself?

---

[11] James M. Buchanan, *The Limits of Liberty: Between Anarchy and Leviathan* (Chicago: University of Chicago Press, 1975), p. 149.